ALL ROADS LEAD TO KENMARE.

by

STANLEY EDWARD GODDARD

Originally written in

1983

TRAFFORD
PUBLISHING

...for anyone who ever walked all the way over there
Just to see what over here looked like...
Or who climbed anything because it was there...

Note for Librarians: A cataloguing record for this book is available from Library and Archives Canada at www.collectionscanada.ca/amicus/index-e.html
ISBN 1-4120-8676-0

Printed in Victoria, BC, Canada. Printed on paper with minimum 30% recycled fibre. Trafford's print shop runs on "green energy" from solar, wind and other environmentally-friendly power sources.

TRAFFORD
PUBLISHING™

Offices in Canada, USA, Ireland and UK

Book sales for North America and international:
Trafford Publishing, 6E–2333 Government St.,
Victoria, BC V8T 4P4 CANADA
phone 250 383 6864 (toll-free 1 888 232 4444)
fax 250 383 6804; email to orders@trafford.com
Book sales in Europe:
Trafford Publishing (UK) Limited, 9 Park End Street, 2nd Floor
Oxford, UK OX1 1HH UNITED KINGDOM
phone 44 (0)1865 722 113 (local rate 0845 230 9601)
facsimile 44 (0)1865 722 868; info.uk@trafford.com
Order online at:
trafford.com/06-0432

10 9 8 7 6 5 4 3 2

STANLEY GODDARD was a passionate walker, cyclist, climber and photographer who always considered Kenmare to be his spiritual home, even though he'd been born an Englishman and had lived most of his life in faraway Hampshire. A man who adored the rugged scenery of County Kerry and never fell out of love with the magnificent 'Reeks'. He was never happier than on the days he'd strike out for the mountains with little more than a pair of stout boots, his camera and a packet of sandwiches. Many of the discoveries that he made, the result of countless hours spent traipsing across bog, stream and field in pursuit of 'Butter Rolls' and 'Mushroom rocks' that at times must have seemed like idle follies from folklore or the imagination.. Though he would have been the last to admit it, he had an almost encyclopaedic knowledge of Kenmare, its history and its surrounds. Knew the 'green roads', tracks and lanes as well as anyone and had a passion for the landscape and its rich heritage that was never to be diminished. His very last journey in life being to return 'home' to Kenmare.

STANLEY EDWARD GODDARD died in April 1998 in the Kenmare Hospital and is buried in the old graveyard literally a stone's throw from the Kenmare River and with a fine view of the very mountains that were as much a part of the man as his camera and his typewriter.

PREFACE.

All Roads Lead to Kenmare was originally written in 1983 and as you can imagine a great deal has changed in both the Town and the surrounding area in the intervening period. Were he still alive today I doubt that the author would have recognised some of the buildings he'd photo-graphed over the years, or understood some of the 21st century 'improvements.'

But in spite of everything he would have still recognised the town, known the landscape in which it sits and still have understood what it is that makes Kenmare tick. For history doesn't change, it can't be improved, as we rush headlong into the future the past just gets older and more precious, serving to remind us of where we've been, who we were and why it still matters.

To have updated the book might have seemed like the right thing to do. It would have explained where some things have gone and might well have made other things easier to find. But it would also have deprived the reader of the opportunity to see for themselves how things have changed. For it's only when you appreciate just how much Kenmare has evolved in twenty years that you can truly understand the significance of the previous two hundred.

CONTENTS.

ALL ROADS LEAD TO KENMARE.

by

Stanley Edward Goddard

1925-1998

A Travellers Guide to South Kerry.

In the Irish tongue Kenmare is named 'an Neiden' or the little nest and no other name could be more fitting for this charming, little market town nestling in the ragged heart of County Kerry. Its dramatic location amongst the high mountains, at the head of the mighty Kenmare River making it a welcome haven for any travellers on the roads from Sneem, Killarney or Glengarrif. That you are literally out on the open road one minute and the next in the centre of town, an indication of the impact of the *'little nest'* and the way that Kenmare appears around you before the memories of the mountains have had the chance to fade. Or perhaps before you've had the time to realise that it was coming?

Of all the roads that lead to Kenmare, the approach from Glengarrif is probably the most breath-taking. For after climbing up and over the western reaches of the 'Caha Mountains', and negotiating the famous tunnels cut through the very rock of 'Baurearagh', the traveller rapidly descends into the fertile 'Sheen-River Valley', through Bonane and on towards Tullaha and Ballygriffin. The last few miles into town are tame in comparison. Travelled on a road flanked by tall trees that offer only brief, tantalising, flickering vista's of the imposing heights of 'Mucksna' and 'Knockerika', it would be easy to forget that you are in Kerry. Easy to forget that around here surprises lurk around every corner. For then, all at once, whether the traveller is on foot, bicycle, horseback or using mechanical means, they will very suddenly find themselves on a splendid, double-arched bridge with a panoramic view on either side. On their left and looking East, they will spy the dramatic 'Kenmare Bay' and the distant Atlantic ocean, and on their right, looking West, the tranquil estuary of the 'Roughty River'. A beautiful, natural Harbour known locally as 'The Sound.'

It is a moment to be savoured. The sudden, dramatic change of scenery truly appreciated when, having travelled through the shaded, Sheen-River Valley of 'Ballygriffin', you suddenly emerge into the sunshine, coast onto the bridge and looking to east and west, see water as far as the eye can see. Few travellers fail to be impressed and there aren't too many who fail to stop on the bridge and 'take-in' the views that are hard to forget. The click of a camera's shutter capturing a memory on film that is unlikely to fade in the memory, or lose any of its magic in years to come.

The bridge, an all-concrete structure, except for the stone piers, was built in 1932 and cost just a few pounds shy of £10,000, the skilled workmanship and simple design having withstood both the weather and the test of time for over half a century. Known throughout the surrounding countryside as *'Our Lady's Bridge'*, a great many of the older generation still know it as 'the Sound Bridge. While many more, who are usually just passing through, simply remember it as 'Kenmare Bridge.'

Blessed with a stunning location that not only affords both locals and visitors alike with magnificent views, it is also a bridge that is almost impossible to avoid at some point in a holiday or a working week. As for routes to Glengarrif, Bantry, Castletown-Bearhaven or Kilgarvan there really is no other sensible way. And travellers to Killarney would be hard-pressed to find a by-pass or detour that didn't take them on a veritable 'wild goose chase' o'er hill, valley and Lough!

Though not as old as some 'Kenmare Bridge' is still one of the most pleasant looking, modern bridges built in

Ireland and at the time of its opening was, with two arches spanning over 350 feet, one of the largest of its kind in the whole of the British Isles.

It had replaced the old, 'Lansdowne Suspension Bridge,' which coincidentally had also been the first of its kind to be built in Ireland almost a hundred years before?

Very different to its modern counterpart, this design had allowed the road to be suspended from a central, limestone tower and anchored at both banks by wire hawsers set in strong, bonded stonework. This bridge, built in 1840, had been a joint effort between the 'Board of Works and the 4th Marquis of Lansdowne and funded by a generous grant of £3000 given by the previous Marquis in 1839.

Built a long time before the Motor Car first ventured onto Kerry's highways and by-ways. The old, *'swaying'* bridge, as locals had referred to it, had been widely used by horse-drawn travellers and those on foot for over a hundred years. Either bridge something of a genuine 'God-send', as the only alternatives had been a 4 mile hike 'around Roughty', or to take your chances with a token, ferry service that was very reminiscent of the one on the River Suir in County Waterford, between 'Passage-East' and 'Ballyhack.' A ferry that was still giving good service in 1952.

All that's left of the old bridge these days is the central, limestone pier that supports the new bridge and a few, fine photographs taken 80 years ago by the well known landscape photographer 'W.L.Lawrence.' Many of these can still be seen in the lounge bar of the 'Lansdowne Arms Hotel,' Kenmare's oldest Hotel, which was once an Inn and still sits proudly at the top of town at the junction of Shelbourne Street and Main Street.

New bridge or old, the view has remained the same over the years and on a warm, summer's day the Kenmare Bay, dressed in the still water of low tide and with a gentle haze on the horizon, can give the appearance of it being a huge lake. Over the year's visitors to Kerry have often compared this vast expanse of salt water to a fjord. And as the sun sets, the distant mountains recede into shadow and the fine line between water and sky is blurred by the mist, it is indeed only too easy to be reminded of far off places. But then as you look up and see the last remnants of the light turn Mucksna Mountain from silver grey to chocolate brown. You'll remember that you are in fact in Kenmare and maybe its everywhere else that resembles here?

It is an impressive expanse of water and when you consider that it is over 30 miles long, nearly 5 miles wide at its mouth where it joins the mighty Atlantic Ocean and subject to tidal extremes that can have moored boats battling fierce swells at dawn and yet be all but beached, high and dry at dusk.

The Ordnance Survey map clearly states *'an Ribhear'* or 'Kenmare River' when perhaps Kenmare Bay would seem more fitting. But, whatever description or term suits best, it is almost a certainty that no other river in Ireland has a bridge with two more different stretches of water on either side. But County Kerry, or 'The Kingdom' as it's often more affectionately known, is a place of sometimes epic extremes and Kenmare Bridge with the mighty Atlantic to the west and the humble Roughty to the east is a fine example of what to expect. Or is that what not to expect?

There are many islands in the river, their names as beautiful and dramatic as the Ice age that created them many thousands of years ago. Places like Dunkerron, Greenane, Cappanacush, Illaunakilla and Dronnoge. At the mouth of the Sneem river estuary not too far from Kenmare lay Rosadohan, Sherky and Illaunleagh Islands. Across the river Dinish Island is one of the few that are still inhabited and with its spectacular views of sea and mountains and natural salt-water moat you cannot help but feel that it must be the perfect place for solitude and privacy.

At one time the waters of the Kenmare River abounded with Cod, Hake, Mackerel, Ling, Tope and Herrings. It has also on occasion been home to shoals of Portuguese Man'o Wars, schools of Dolphins and even the occasional Killer Whale that's been known to rub alongside the fishermen's boats before beaching itself by the bridge.

In the 18th Century as many as a hundred boats would regularly fish the abundant waters. But even though Kerry pushes out into the Atlantic at the very edge of western Europe, its boats were never suited to deep-sea fishing and even though the brave men of Castletown-Bere had no qualms about rowing 25 miles out to their fishing grounds in the Atlantic, they were never tempted to venture any further and so it was said, always kept a wary eye on the green land on the horizon.

Being a fertile, tidal estuary, the Kenmare River also abounds in Shellfish, lots of shellfish. This includes fine Lobsters, Oysters, Scallops, Crabs, Mussels and Cockles, most of which can be readily caught no more than 15 miles or so from the famous bridge which itself was once a fine vantage point to see huge shoals of Salmon when the tide was on the ebb. A spot from where you could watch in fascination as local fishermen used net, boat and great skill to catch the freshest of fish under the ever-keen eye of the water bailiff.

But back at the end of the 17th Century, and before either bridge was even thought of; fishing in the Kenmare River was a different story. For back then, in the summer months, it wasn't uncommon to see large numbers of Mottled-Seals all along the rocky shores. Though some remain to this day and are now regarded as a fine sight. In the old days the Seals were regarded as competition and caused many a shortfall in the Salmon nets and to such an extent at one point, that they were deemed a real threat to peoples livelihoods. Since the Salmon was one of the chief local exports, a natural food resource and part of the staple income of many local people, it was decided that something had to be done.

The choice was obvious, but the locals had no means of killing the Seals while they were in the water and any attempt at catching them in strong nets proved futile as the Seals strong teeth were more than a match for anything that the fishermen had at their disposal.

The only viable alternative was to try and kill the Seals while they were on dry-land. This involved clambering over the rocks and trying to shoot them in the head with a musket. Though there were proper 'Seal-Catchers' who would catch the young Seals by moonlight in the coastal caverns. Their services came at a price that some thought too high. Seal Catchers were not highly thought of; even though it was a job with real risks as mother Seals could be especially fierce when it came to defending their offspring. Their habit of never letting go of whatever they bit into until it cracked or broke between their jaws, making the Seal-Catchers a rare breed in every sense of the word!

But, if the risks were high, so were the rewards. The oil from a dead Seal boiled down was worth anything up to fifty shillings and when you compared this to the average wage of the workmen who built 'Our Lady's Bridge', who got just forty shillings per week, you could understand why men were prepared to take their chances against a creature weighing as much as a small horse. Their only protection being their quick wits and some primitive body armour that consisted of sacking filled with quilted charcoal tied to their arms.

Nowadays, though there are still some Seals to be seen in the river, their numbers are much reduced, as are the fish stocks that have been drastically depleted by the sort of over-fishing that is the result of too many factory Trawlers catering for foreign markets. But there are still plenty of fish in the River and against the odds; some have created records in the Angling world. One such fish being a Skate weighing 218 pounds and a huge Halibut that was 5 foot in length, 3 foot wide and weighed over 153 pounds! Both fish incidentally landed on rod and line by a very proud Mr.Henning.

It is also possible when the summers are more settled, to see large shoals of Mackerel that have left the Atlantic and headed up the river as far as the bridge. Whether by accident or design, such an occasion could prove to be a bountiful one for local children. Who, using the bridge as a pontoon, and with just a simple spinner on a hand-line, could easily catch the fleeting fish as they darted under the double arches. Reaping an unexpected, natural harvest that could be easily sold to country people on their journey homeward. Two fine, fresh Mackerel satisfying both Angler and customer for just one shilling.

For the non-angler the Mackerel was no less interesting, for onlookers could stand and watch the still waters beyond the pier, waiting for what could appear to resemble a sheet of glass being shattered as the hungry Mackerel boiled to the surface in pursuit of the Sprats they fed on. The waters bubbling like a boiling saucepan as nature lived out its cycle and envious anglers looked on.

Such a phenomenon was usually tied to unusual weather or tidal conditions and have become something of a rarity in recent years, for like many parts of the British Isles, the climate in and around Kerry has changed quite dramatically over the years and unfortunately for Kenmare in particular, these changes seem to be for the worse.

Just thirty years ago the summers were long and hot and while yes, you would always get that odd, heavy shower to come rolling in from the Atlantic on an August afternoon to drench the unfortunate walker or cyclist. A few moments later the clouds would recede, the sun would re-appear and in just a quarter of an hour, he or she would be bone-dry and gasping for a drink. And it wasn't just the summers that were better and drier. They were also a lot longer, often creeping into Autumn and occasionally even Winter too, so that even in the middle of December it wasn't so uncommon for locals to enjoy a bit of modest sun-bathing while they watched the Seals basking on the rocks.

Though it might sound a little far-fetched, it wouldn't be so unreasonable to suggest that Kenmare practically had a climate of its own at one time. Certainly in the days when the Seal-culling was at its height, it was often noticed that during the months of August, September and October there was a balmy-softness in the air that combined with a rare freshness in the atmosphere that was unheard of in Ireland or the rest of the British Isles. It was reputed to make the climate more delightful in summer and considerably more temperate for seven or eight months of the year.

A reason for this temperate climate was undoubtedly the 'Gulf Stream', a warm current of water that originates in the Gulf of Mexico and crosses the Atlantic, where it eventually separates into two distinct currents. One of these currents striking full upon the bay of Kenmare, about 26 miles from the bridge. Here the charged, rain clouds hit the mountains on each side of the river. The 'Slieve Miskish' range to the south-east and the 'Reeks' to the north and bring rain as they float inland from the ocean. Many a time as you watch shower after shower breaking on the distant hills, all is sunshine in the town of Kenmare. The warm Even balmy temperatures, a pleasant contrast to the cooler climes along the banks of the bay.

So-called weather experts have often predicted that every seventh year brings a really hot summer to Ireland as a whole. In County Kerry in 1976 and 1983 this was borne out by scorching temperatures and extremely low rainfall, but hasn't always been as reliable as that of the Farmers, who can look at the sky and offer a visitor a forecast that is not only accurate, but sometimes good for nine or ten days hence.

Failing that, as many an Irish grandmother has uttered before now, "if you want to know the weather, then look out of the window boy!"

Sound advice indeed...

CHAPTER TWO.

Kenmare is probably one of the best towns in the south-west for tourists to use as a base for their holiday. It's truly central location making it an ideal place for anyone touring Kerry and West-Cork or well placed for anyone who's just lucky enough to live there. The Town's unique geography meaning that it's perfectly poised just off the 'Ring of Kerry, but also sat perfectly at the gateway to the rugged 'Ring of Beara. On a simply practical level, the famous bridge also means that the 'Little Nest' is well within comfortable striking distance of Cork, Killarney, Glengarrif, Bantry, Tralee and even Waterville, Valentia Island and the 'Skelligs.'

The town is also not without importance in other areas. As long ago as 1302, a Papal Taxation gave special preference to *'Eccia de Keynmara'*, which some believe might be the original name of the town. Whatever the case, it clearly shows that Kenmare was fairly well known even then and these days, the 'Little Nest' can certainly boast all the necessary amenities for tourists whatever their nationality. While the rugged scenery with its unique shades of light and dark have never had a problem being translated into any tongue.

Though not technically a big town, Kenmare is blessed with a generous mixture of shops and facilities that offer both practicality and quality.

On Main Street for example there is a well organised launderette and a restaurant under the same roof. So that anyone paying for a 'service wash' is able to 'kill two birds with one stone and partake of a fine meal, knowing full well that after the 'Irish Stew' and Apple Pie and cream, your clean, dry washing will all be ready for your collection. A simple enough idea, it is one that is much better than those offered in many larger towns and one that saves the would be launderer from endless hours fretting about 'enough change' and staring dementedly at the tumble dryer, that always takes a veritable lifetime to complete its cycle, leaving the launderer, agitated, broke and usually hungry!

Unusual for even some of the larger provincial towns, there is even a decent, public toilet all but under the shadow of the spire of the 'Holy-Cross Church.' Something that is not just of benefit to the tourist 'passing through', but also something of a 'God-send' for those sinners who can't quite manage a long service without a 'little nip outside to water the flowers.' A simple enough amenity and one that is as such taken for granted, but is maybe not as common as you might think?

The two, chief thoroughfares through town are the afor-mentioned Main Street and Henry Street, both of which converge on 'The Square', which technically speaking isn't a square at all, but the main intersection and bottom point of a large triangle. The remaining side made up by Shelbourne Street which runs along the very top of town joining the other two sides and roads together. If it were possible to look out of a helicopter hovering directly overhead, the layout of the town would probably resemble an airfield. With the wider Main Street as the runway, Shelbourne street as the perimeter and Henry Street as the main taxi-way.

Though unusual, the design of the town is no accident and strangely enough, thanks to Sir William Petty, the Earl of Shelbourne, a very 'English' design. The Square especially giving the impression of an English Village green without the ornamental railings and the wide street opposite all too easily mistaken for a village market place complete with stalls.

The large trees in the square have also provided homes for many generations of Crows. Their rude calls echoing throughout the town from early morning to late evening, reminding all who passed through or who lived in Kenmare that they were perhaps the original residents of the town and as such have as much of a claim to the streets, trees and rooftops as any Kerry-man or woman.

In latter years the square as also become something of a haven for hikers and cyclists who can escape the heavily-motorised tourist traffic for a while and enjoy a well-earned rest and a snack before hopping back into the saddle and continuing along their weary way.

While Main Street, or 'William Street' as it was known at the turn of the century, is very, very wide with enough room for visitors to park 'nose-in' on both sides and still leave two good size lanes for through traffic. Henry Street most definitely is not. In stark comparison it's narrow, very narrow and unlike Main Street, two rows of conventional kerb-side parking can often leave precious little space for anyone trying to get through, never mind linger outside their favourite pub or restaurant , of which incidentally there are just a few.

Shelbourne Street at the top of town is of similar width, but with fewer shops and business's is generally pretty accessible much of the time. All these streets are by the way, one way and so progress through Kenmare is, shall we say 'steady' certainly quick enough for anyone in all but a frantic hurry, but slow enough to afford the patient visitor plenty of time to peruse an impressive selection of shops, both old and new. The majority of which were built around the turn of the century, though there are a few of a much later date.

Of the limestone buildings in Henry Street, one particularly good example is *'JACK TANGNEY'S'*, its large windows and relatively un-touched interiors retaining all the quaint character and atmosphere of the 'good old days', but without any of that museum-like stuffiness, as the shop itself still serves the local farming community with a large range of small tools and implements that are necessary for day to day work and especially useful for those who still cut their 'turf' by hand. A skill that is rare, but once again on the increase because of the high cost of oil and imported coal.

It will be a very sad day when these delightful, old places succumb to the pressures of modern business and go 'under the hammer'. The fate of the fine, old buildings put in the hands of builders and property developers who seldom have any regard for heritage or tradition.

But such is life, just being quaint, a local landmark, or having always been there, is never going to be enough to justify their survival, never mind allow them to compete with market forces and as many people still flock to the wilds of Kerry and vie for a chance to live in the beautiful scenery, so the pressure on the past will increase and just as surely, so the Estate Agents will come. That there are currently 6 in the town, all within 10 minutes walk of each other, proof if any were needed, of just how things are perhaps to become in the years to come. Certainly since the advent of Ireland's entry into the Common Market in 1968, German and Dutch visitors alone have bought up over 2000 acres of prime Kerry soil. Their interest and the demand it creates pushing up the prices of even the most humble homestead. Like they say, 'time and tide wait for no man' and neither would it seem, does mans need to make more money!

But money isn't everything and no self respecting Irish town, Village, Hamlet, Parish or crossroads would be complete without its Public Bar. The way in which they often seem the very hub of Irish life itself, defining their worth and their significance to a community that lives hard, works hard, prays hard and just happens to be partial to a wee drop of the 'old, black stuff' from time to time. Just to quench the thirst mind, or 'wet' a dry throat.

But often the bars are more than just 'pubs', more than just somewhere to drink or talk or enjoy 'the Craic.' They are also a haven, an office, a refuge, even a confessional and undoubtedly the scene of many a business deal, many a bout of hard-bargaining and many a glass of 'Guinness, when hands are shook and deals are considered 'done.'

Yes, it can also be the same place where shirts are lost, shepherds are fleeced, profits and indeed wages are supped away. But such is the nature of business, the lure of the 'black stuff' and indeed, the very weakness of men.

For many 'Guinness' is as Irish as Ireland itself and when Sir Benjamin Lee Guinness founded his world famous firm in the 19th Century, he probably couldn't have known just how popular his creation would become.

For those who don't know, the drink itself is a very strong ale or stout, with an inky black colour and the distinctive creamy white head that has been the subject of much speculation, debate and even some fisticuffs over the years. For if it was decided that the Guinness wasn't up to standard, it wasn't unknown for a bar to be abandoned by its clientele until a new barman, a new delivery or even a change of management put things right!

And it wasn't just about how the stout was kept. For years the pouring of the perfect pint has assumed an almost reverential significance and is considered by many to be a craft that only comes with years of devoted practice, the precise proportion of head and Stout a benchmark that can make or break a reputation. For the uninitiated the time it takes to pour the pint in two separate stages, can be confusing but after your first taste it all becomes very clear, that 'all good things come to those who wait.'

The Irish take their drinking seriously and 'The Guinness' is a drink that matters, a drink to be anticipated as much as it's savoured, and as anyone who's tasted a genuine 'Irish pint' in the 'Atlantic Bar' on a hot August night knows, there's nothing quite like it on Gods green earth!

Mind you before Ireland's famous stout became the drink of choice, Cider was just what the doctor ordered. Irish apples producing a type of Cider that was known locally as 'Cockygoes' and was reputed to be almost as strong as another drink, that is apparently called 'Poteen' and produced in the mountains. Or so I'm told.

Though not an especially large town, Kenmare can offer the discerning drinker no fewer than 23 licensed Public Houses, ranging in style from a 5 star Hotel to the traditionally quaint one-room bar and shop, which in some cases haven't changed in over a century.

It's a simple bit of Irish logic, being able to buy your Corn Flakes, spuds and a drop of stout at the same time and under the same roof, an idea that should be preserved for practical and historical reasons. It would be a great pity to see these old style Bars disappear, the loss of a hostelry where people could still enjoy a drink in peace and quiet, without the intrusion of modern music or the dreaded 'fruit-machines', would be a great one. And while these bars might not prove such a draw for the summer tourists thirsting after 'the Craic.' On those long winter's nights when all the visitors are long gone, there should still be somewhere for the senior citizens of the town to go and cool their heels and reminisce about days past. Grand times when the world wasn't quite so busy, so expensive or so loud!

Only just outside the town are two highly recommended Hotels, both offering very good cuisine and a warm welcome for visiting families.

'The Great Southern' is a fine old, traditional, 'country-house' style of Hotel; set in a grand, old building that's very reputation suggests service, quality and tradition.

Then there is 'The Riversdale' which is more modern in style and the amenities it has on offer, but no less hospitable and comforting for the weary traveller. In the evenings these Hotels, like many of the Bars in Town can often offer fine musical entertainment in the true Irish tradition. The fiddle, tin whistle, or the lively, Button-Accordion quite often providing the foot-tapping tunes for many a jig or reel.

'The Lansdowne' is Kenmare's oldest public house and as you would expect maintains the great tradition of Irish music and ballads. The landlord Bobby Hanley, a very popular host, as well as being a lively contributor to the enjoyment of his customers on their night out. Young and old savouring the very best of Irish hospitality and not just in the evenings.

In 1983, for perhaps the first time in Kenmare, Bobby started Mini-Bus, tourist trips. Every weekend a different adventure to places like; The Ring of Kerry, The Dingle and Beara Peninsula's and Killarney. Much in demand from the older folks, it was also a rare chance for the motorist to have a day off and enjoy the charm and wit of Bobby as both driver and Courier. His charming commentary as he navigated the wild roads, well worth the ticket price on its own.

While on the subject of drink, though not the alcoholic variety I should say. Half way along Market Street, which once housed the Town's fire station, is an old, water appliance. No relation to the Fire Engine, that is better known as 'the pump' and was at one time the only means by which the tenants of the adjoining cottages could benefit from a water supply, as it was not until 1955 that mains water was finally laid beneath the street.

Though obviously a great benefit to the good people of Market Street, its long overdue arrival was not without certain risks, as the only way to excavate the rock for the pipe work was by blasting underground. To minimise damage, before laying the dynamite, Council workmen covered all the doors and windows of the neat, little cottages with corrugated, iron sheets. Though crude, it was a system that proved very effective and no damage was recorded and soon the tenants were able to enjoy the luxury of running water indoors for the first time, the old pump suddenly finding itself little more than an antique.

And it's still there, along with several of its companions around the town. One outside the 'Gardai' station in Shelbourne Street and another on Bridge Street looking towards the Reeks. Now a cul-de-sac, Bridge Street was once a short but busy roadway with fordable access across the Finnihy Rover and a direct route to Sneem.

Meanwhile, back on the corner of Market Street where it joins the Square is a well-preserved, Limestone building with a pitched slate roof called the 'Market House.' It is reputed to have been built in 1795 and boats a unique set of doorways and windows with a round style that is very much at odds to the rest of the town, where conventional rectangular is the norm'. An imposing building with a good, corner plot, it's a fine place to view the Square and to pass the time of day. Doing as perhaps many of Kenmare's older citizens have done through-out the years, just watching the world go by and picking up all the latest news on that large, flag-stoned corner and it has to be said, usually a good few days before the local paper!

To the right of this attractive building, there is a gateway that was once used by horses from the mail and passenger cars. Here they were led through to be watered and fed, 'four in hand' before continuing on with their journey. But by the 1950's the stables were long gone and since Kenmare was yet to be hooked up to the County electricity supply, the stalls and troughs were replaced with a private generating plant that gave good service to many of the town's business's and a few private houses. Though there were occasions when the generator broke down and the posh bulbs would fade into darkness, it was never for very long. On these rare emergency's the posh people would just have to make do with candles and oil lamps like the rest of the good town's people.

Then as now, most of the shops in the town were painted in soft colours that would contrast, rather than clash with their neighbours, bars and shops sporting the family name in bold but simple sign writing. Establishing a style of country town 'chic' that is still very much in evidence to this day.

Still in Market Street and on the same side as 'Market House' stands a row of Victorian Cottages built in 1891. Though humble by today's standards they are very quaint and neat and well kept by the proud tenants who can step from their front door onto the pavement. Across the street stand a fine row of terraced houses, that with their carved and decorated eaves and gables are perhaps more reminiscent of a Country Railway station. The fronts of the houses boasting well-tended gardens that are a blaze of colour in the spring and summer.

All in all, it gives Market Street an interesting and contrasting demeanour, the Victorian Cottages more 'Irish' than perhaps the railway Cottages with their 'English flower gardens. But Kenmare, as many visitors have noticed over the years, has a peculiarly 'English ' feel which is of no surprise when you think that it was an Englishman, John Petty-Fitzmaurice the 1st Marquis of Lansdowne that planned the town in 1775, based on a design that was then known as the 'X' plan. It gave the town its peculiar triangulation and a lot of features that make Kenmare a rarity, though if a traveller were keen to find something more familiar.

They would be hard pushed to find a more 'Irish' street than Market Street.

It's an Irish thoroughfare through and through. Even though, yes it is technically a cul-de-sac and doesn't have any shops, it's Kenmare all over, the characteristic dwellings as different and individual as many of the older citizens that have lived there for many years, and certainly long enough to still remember it as Pound Lane. And it would have been as Pound Lane that this particular street would have laid claim to its real significance, the days when it was as important as many of the other, wider, longer, busier streets and in an era where horse and donkey still outnumbered cars ten to one, the home of two of the most important craftsmen in the town, The Blacksmith and the Wheelwright.

It was probably a logical, sensible situation that brought two such businesses' so close together, each one directly dependant on the other for as many reasons as there were carts to build and repair, and horses and donkey's to shoe. If they were still there it would certainly be a fine excuse for the visitor to forego the scenery for a while and appreciate the making of a wheel carved from Ash-wood, or watch the finishing touches being applied to a Turf-Cart via a fine coat of red-lead paint. Back then these sturdy, little vehicles were the main source of transport for everything from Winter-fuel and kindling, to crops and livestock, churns of milk and cream and even people on the long haul back out to the farms.

But of all the trades, it was probably the wheelwright who was more respected as a craftsman, and rightly so. The skill required to make a wheel was a combination of carpentry, geometry and metalworking. The turning of 19 pieces of timber and some iron into a beautiful, practical, functional tool, a true art form when the tools were in the hands of a craftsman like Paddy Corkery.

Here was a man who knew that the timber had to be

well-seasoned; neither swelled by rain or shrunk by sun, but a fine piece of mature Ash-wood, Beech or Oak, for if it wasn't the wheel would be of no use to man nor beast. Construction was a well practised process. First the six rims were made of Ash-wood or Beech, each mortised to take two spokes and be able to form a perfect circle when joined together. The spokes, always an even number, were shaped from oak with a spoke shave. The hub or knave, made of seasoned Elm was the most important element in the construction, its positioning and strength the key to a good wheel or the having to start all over. The mortising on the hub was performed with the utmost skill, the spokes had to be equi-distant from each other, parallel but not at right angles to the axle. For strength they had to be at just the right angle, this gave the wheel its dish shape and its strength. The smallest inaccuracy in cutting the mortises would spoil the wheel and the 'driving home' of the spokes with a mighty sledgehammer was always a tense moment. The precision of the joints meant that the spokes would be immovable and so there was no leeway between right and wrong, they were one or the other. Wrong was a waste of many hours work, right meant that the wheel went to the blacksmith for the fitting of the iron tyre.

First the Smith would measure the circumference of the wheel with a 'Traveller', a tool that ensured the marking out of a perfect circle, then he would cut, shape and weld the iron before heating it to just the right temperature in the forge. Finally the tyre would be hammered onto the wheel red hot, and then cooled in a bath. The tyre giving the wheel its strength and protecting the wood from the rough roads, for without the Blacksmith's experience all the wheelwright's skill would be wasted.

But times have changed and due to the rise of the infernal motor car, all three of the Town's Blacksmiths and also the wheelwright are all long gone, their forges now derelict and their skills redundant. For Market Street it is a sad loss, as never again will the sweet aroma of wood-shavings, or the bray and neigh of horses and donkeys being shoed, fill the air or sweeten the kitchens of the cottages on a soft Kerry day.

Away from the memories, the bottom end of Market Street climbs gently towards the old, stone circle, or 'Bobby's Rocks' as they're known locally. Here the houses are older and more basic in construction from the cottages at the prettier end of the street. Three lime-washed dwellings form a terrace of one-up, one-down's, two small windows in front and none at the back, a large open hearth with a proper flue and chimney in the kitchen-cum-living room and rough, rustic stairs up to one bedroom. It's a basic design and a basic construction, the solid twelve inch thick walls having no other decoration other than the lime wash inside and out. It's simple white, and easy to maintain, bright and according to the *'Board of Health'*, something of a cleanser, which was a good prevention against disease. The Board didn't worry too much that there was no water and no sanitation in the property, but then compared to the cabins of the previous century, these humble homes were practically luxurious.

Back in the 19th Century, the bulk of ordinary folk lived in 'Cabins'. These were basic, one room buildings with a huge hearth and a hard, rough floor made of natural cement. Furniture was fairly scarce as timber was much in demand for Sir William Petty's greedy iron furnaces and important or delicate articles like Tea or Tobacco were stored in holes in the walls. Staples like Oatmeal and flour stored in sturdy wooden bins made by the wheelwright.

The open hearth was the main focus of the home in every way, not just for heat and light and comfort but also because it was where all the cooking was done. The baking with the help of a 'crane and crook or a pot-oven called 'A

Bastable', or with the griddle hung over the crane with live embers of turf on top for all-round heat.

The food was basic but hearty fare; oaten bread made at the edge of the fire and of course potatoes cooked in their skins in a three legged, iron pot. At meal times the family would all sit around the fire. If times were good, milk, onions, vegetables even home-made butter would be added to the spuds, turning a simple baked potato into delicious 'colcannon'.

The old, lime washed cottages of Market Street are perhaps some of the oldest in the town of Kenmare. Though no records exist of when they were built, it can be reckoned that they were at least a hundred and fifty years old give or take a decade, and while yes they were about as basic and rudimentary as a home could be without plumbing or sanitation, of the most utilitarian one-up, one –down design and almost totally lacking in most of the plush home comforts and furnishings we take for granted these days. They were, despite the lack of facilities, 'proper family homes' where, with the oil-lamp glowing and the turf-fire blazing, there existed a true atmosphere of simplicity and homeliness that many might be happy to go back to in these greedy, hectic times.

Most of Kenmare was built in the mid 19th Century when the population of the town was around just 1,200. At this time local exports were largely Corn, Salmon, butter and of course, sheep and cattle, while coal, timber and ironstone were the main goods to be imported. Or at least they were the most popular, legal, imports, as smuggling accounted for almost as much in terms of goods and could provide the local gentry with fine French Brandy, Claret, silks and Dutch cigars. It also provided many local people with a reasonable living from contraband traffic as rich, Irish wool fetched good returns in French ports and French ships were frequents visitors to Killmakilloge and Ardgroom harbours in the Kenmare River and the nearby Bantry Bay.

Eventually, the British Authorities in Dublin Castle got wind of the illicit trade and despatched Revenue Cutters, manned by His Majesty's Customs and Excise men. But the waters of Kenmare Bay were more familiar to the French and Irish sailors who had a smugglers knowledge of the tides, currents and the many small islands in and around Killmakilloge and Ardgroom's natural harbours. Here they were able to load and unload their cargos on any of the smuggler's coves that existed on the likes of 'Spanish Island', 'Bird Island', 'Black Island 'or even 'Pig Island, and all too easily elude the customs men.

For more 'legal' cargo's there was also 'The Pier' situated a stone's throw from the bridge and built in 1826, it was reputed to be the first of its kind in Kerry and was deemed 'an excellent construction with an ideal length that gave ample anchorage for any sailing boats, ships and even Coastal Tramp-steamers when there was a need'. The 'Derricks' on the ships meant that cargo's could be unloaded straight onto the horse and carts. A time saving practice that could be very beneficial on occasion, and especially if the Customs men were abroad.

During the 1930's when the losses of Steam Trawlers in the Atlantic off the south-west coast of Ireland were especially heavy, it was not uncommon for Trawlers to take shelter at the pier and ride out the fierce Atlantic squalls that would roar up the Kenmare Bay and rattle the Beech trees by the pier-side cottages to their very roots!

But though the pull of the sea has always been strong in Kenmare, the fields of Dromnevane and Cleady were just as fertile. Apart from cattle and sheep, the main local crops were Oats and Barley-Grain and the main tool used in the cultivation and harvest was the 'long handled spade' which can still be purchased in *'O'Brien-Corkery's'* and is still widely used. While oats were a relatively straightforward task for the farmer, Barley Grain had to be pulled off the straw with the fingers then put in the loft to dry for a 'good, long while'. Only then could the good, old long-handled spade be put to good use shovelling the dry barley into a barrel where the grain was separated from the chaff, the process completed only when the grain was hung to dry in two sheets suspended from the rafters.

Another vital job at harvest time, the 'saving of the hay' had always been a trying time for farmers. A good crop of fine, winter silage totally dependant on the cruel, unpredictable weather and the farmers' judgement in 'bringing it in', in time, but not so soon that it hadn't had the chance to dry out properly. To this day it is the judgement and experience of man that 'saves or loses the hay', technology reassuringly absent from the decision process and in parts of Kerry missing from the process altogether. Despite modern practices and baling machines, the process of turning the scythed hay by hand can still be seen in the fields and farms around Kenmare. As can the old practice of tying a waterproof sheet on top of the haycock to act as a roof, giving the hay a few extra days drying that could be vital to the success of this winter's fodder.

It is also still possible in the age of diesel Tractors to see yet another way of saving the hay. The *'Tumbling Paddy'* was a 10ft wooden beam with a row of iron spikes on either side that was pilled behind a horse and left the hay in neat rows for drying. Even in 1983 it's possible to see such practises still in use, and to see a *'tumbling Paddy'* being pulled by a donkey in the Glastrasna Valley near Lauragh on a fine summers day is like stepping back a hundred years and glimpsing another, gentler, quieter and more patient world.

CHAPTER THREE.

O'Brien Corkery's – Byre Dwellings – Derreen House-The Two Churches.

Adding to the 'English' look' of the town and contrary to what many visitors might expect, practically all of the buildings in Kenmare are not thatched like all those 'twee' postcards we've all seen. But are in fact covered with slate, a much more durable, practical and economical resource that hails from local quarries and seems to befit the rugged, practicality of a working town. Though some might see the slate as crude and dour, it does the job and has done on most properties in the Baronies of Iveragh, Glanerought, Dunkerron, and indeed most of County Kerry since about 1700.

Though the slate, it could be said, adds a drab conformity to the rooftops of Kenmare, below the roofline the architecture is full of quirks and variations. One such anomaly is about halfway along Henry Street. Known locally as 'underneath the arches', (no relationship to Flanagan and Allen's immortal song) they sit between two buildings, creating an interesting pair of views and through one you can find one of the first, stone houses to have been built in 'Neiden'. A perfect example of a two storey town house, covered with hand-hewn slates. Situated at the rear of the *'Shamrock Inn'* it is now used as a store and out-house by the adjacent shops. The other arch leads you through to the back door of the largest shop and store in Kenmare; *'DANIEL O'BRIEN CORKERY & COMPANY'* Importers and Merchants.

It is the sort of old fashioned emporium that sells just about anything you're likely to need; Groceries, Draperies, Hardware and General Fancy goods. Everything for the humble housewife who might pop in every other day, to the itinerant farmer who might only come to town once a month. In days past 'O'Brien Corkery's' also provided another service for local people. As the pre-war posters for the 'WHITE STAR LINE' remind, this was the main travel office for the local area and the first port of call, and indeed the first step for many of the immigrants that left County Kerry to seek their fortunes in America. It was possible, in this fine store to book passage on magnificent liners such as the 'Mauritania' and the ill-fated 'Lusitania'. Then it would be the road to Cork City, on to Queenstown, Cobh and out to sea, next stop New York, Boston or Quebec. It was a daunting journey in those days and by no means one that guaranteed the fortune the immigrants sought. For even though many found success in the East River docks and the fine houses of Manhattan, just as many failed and ended up destitute on the hard pavements of the Bowery and Hell's kitchen. But emigration has always been a big part of the Irish Diaspora, relatives in the States or across the water in England are largely commonplace and the eagerly anticipated parcels from America were always as much a part of the Irish way of life as Market day and the soft, Kerry rain.

There was precious little that could not be purchased in this emporium. Whether it was building materials, coal, timber, paint, tools, long-handled spades, shovels and forks for the hay making. They also sold shoes of all sizes and styles, groceries, furniture and even wallpaper. Inside the imposing shop, the main wooden counter was the full length of the ground floor, running from front door to back. Overhead, wires suspended from the high ceiling ran to all the cashiers kiosks and offices like a steel, spider's web. They allowed the sales assistants to despatch money, cheques and requests to the Main Cashier via a small cast iron cup with a screw lid, and the cashier in turn to return receipts and the change back to the customers. It was a simple, logical system and because all money transactions were carried out by one man, mistakes were few and far between, and the system, despite its 'Heath-Robinson' appearance was surprisingly quick.

Unfortunately, these days the wires, the cups and the cashier's kiosk are all long gone, as are most of the staff, the sailing tickets and a lot of the merchandise. Though the shop is the same size it ever was and the four members of staff offer a fine, efficient service they are no match for the likes of John Tuohy and his female assistant who were always good for a laugh and a joke and made shopping in '*O'Brien Corkery's*' something more than a mere trip to the shops.

Across Main Street opposite the front of the emporium is Rock Lane a quiet, little cul-de-sac with a delightful row of picturesque cottages, all with lovely, bright gardens and wooden 'hit and miss' fences. The simple fact that there is barely room for a donkey and cart to turn around never mind a motor car, allowing the lane to retain its character and 'olde worlde' charm.

At the time when the Lansdowne Suspension Bridge was being erected in 1840, it was generally accepted that there were four classes of houses, not just in Kerry but in the whole of Ireland.

The lowest class were the cabins. Windowless, one room dwellings with no chimneys and mud floors that were little more than shelters for the poor families and their animals. As many as ten or even twelve children and just a few sticks of furniture vying for space with a couple of cows who, it was the custom, to milk indoors and let in, through one door and out through the other. These Cabins were very similar to the '*Byre Dwellings*' with animals at one end and people at the other. At night the cattle bedded down on straw and the people, if they were lucky crowded into the simple beds in the best way that they could. The only rule being that the oldest girls slept on the inside next to the wall, and any visitors or relatives hovered precariously on the edges.

The *'Byre Dwellings'* were a better class of habitation than the mud cabin in that they boasted two rooms, a bedroom and a kitchen. Still very primitive and basic, with the same mud floors as the Cabins, they were spared the joy of sharing with the livestock. And had the added bonus of another bedroom that could sometimes be added in the loft space of the roof. Once again, furniture was very scarce, maybe a small table and a settle in the kitchen, and beds made of planks nailed together in the bedroom. The settle was a popular item as a good one could seat as many as five or six people, and it was more comfortable than the short legged chairs and three-legged stools called *'creepies'*. In Sir William Petty's days, cups, platters, bowls and spoons were made of wood and it wasn't until 1800 that iron vessels were eventually replaced with brass.

Besides the light from the turf fire, the only source of light was the *'Cruise Lamp'* a pear-shaped oil lamp made of iron, with a twisted cloth wick lying along the spout or lip. The fuel used was usually fish-oil, but could just as easily be vegetable oil, tallow, lard or even butter. This style of lamp had been in use in various forms since prehistoric times, lamps made of sea-shells having been discovered in coastal areas locally and it was still widely used at the end of the 19th Century.

Because timber was very much in demand for use in the iron industry, stone was the obvious choice for the next class of dwelling. A more sturdy and substantial building but still very much single storey and still with only two or three rooms and the bare minimum of windows. This was down to the window or 'Typhus Tax' that had been imposed in Ireland in the 18th century and wasn't withdrawn until the 19th. It made glass an expensive option and consequently left a lot of people in the dark as the only other cheap alternative was dried, sheep skins.

As building methods progressed through into the 20th Century, a lot of these old stone houses were just abandoned and yet, because of their fine construction still remain to this day. There are some particularly fine examples by the 'old road' just past the Kenmare Hospital and it would certainly be of historical interest to preserve some of those older dwellings as reminders of those unfortunates who eked out a humble existence in years gone by. They would, I feel, be fitting monuments to the hungry years and perhaps all the more authentic for their original location, set amongst the landscape that shaped the lives and fortunes of their inhabitants.

A stones throw from the Holy Cross Church and almost hidden from Railway Road, is Scarteen Park. A modern housing development that unlike many examples elsewhere is a credit to the planners. The houses and bungalows laid out in such a way that none of the homes look out on each other, but instead have a fine view of the trees that give the estate shelter from the east winds. The land the houses are built on was once owned by the 'Southern and Western Railway Company' and was given to the Town council for the purpose of building.

Along the eastern edge of Scarteen Park runs the Kealnagower Stream, no more than a gentle trickle in summer, it can assume the proportions of a raging torrent in winter, and if it is indeed 'in flood' unfortunately so are some of the bungalows at the entrance to the estate likely to be. A situation that it is unfortunate but unavoidable when nature and geography get together.

Close by are the two bridges over which you must travel to enter Scarteen Park. The first is a modern, rudimentary concrete structure that does the job it's meant to do and the second half-hidden by bushes is a picturesque stone bridge that has been doing the same job for two hundred years, but still manages to enhance its surroundings in the way that old structures who weren't just built to last, but built to be looked at as well tend to do. On the opposite bank of the stream high on a rocky ridge and totally obscured from the road by undergrowth stands a stone tower, about ten feet in diameter and possibly twenty five feet high. It's an impressive structure and looks about the same age as a stone arch that was discovered near the concrete bridge about ten years ago. Though it seems to have links with the two hundred year old bridge, at the time of writing no-one seems to know of anything that connects bridge, arch and tower or what the actual purpose of the tower was or, as some locals claim, that it was just a folly.

Returning to Market Street, about halfway down on the left is a lane that at one time of day would have taken you past the old forge to the '*ARCADIA*' Cinema. Though once a thriving part of town, with the Cinema long since closed and the adjacent cottages empty and crumbling this part of Kenmare has a 'ghost-town' feel about it. The two rows of houses are about as basic as you could get, with no outlook , no front garden , and the small backyard barely big enough for a dustbin never mind a washing line or a stack of logs or turf.

With the cottages vacated as recently as the sixties, as they sit and await the bulldozers it's not so hard to perhaps remember them as they once might have been on a gloomy autumn night with the whole family gathered to kneel on the hard stone floor to recite the rosary with the oil lamp turned down. Sombre faces remembering sons and daughters, brothers and sisters that had emigrated to England and America to ease the family burden. The money they would send home to help make ends meet a welcome glimmer of hope in a long, dark winter and a hard, hard life.

When it was open, the *'ARCADIA'* cinema gave three performances a week, except of course if there was a mission in the church, for then Hollywood took second place to God and the manager knew better than to incur the wrath of the Parish Priest who would have frowned on such blasphemy.

For a small town, the *'ARCADIA* was a popular and relatively inexpensive source of entertainment for all ages. A ticket was just sixpence and it was usually a packed house for the one performance every other evening. And packed meant just that, because when all available seats were full, it was quite commonplace for chairs from the booking office to be set up in the aisles. The 'Arcadia' never turned anyone away and was a veritable goldmine for the little shop and bakery next door that sold more bags of sweets and cigarettes in the half hour before a show than it did all day.

At the blocked end of Market Street, off a little side road through an old, iron gate is the old, Lime kiln overlooking the Finnihy River. Although the flames have long since gone out, the stone structure remains in good condition. The two lime quarries that once served the kiln are close by, even though they now boast a fine covering of nature's mantle of grass and bushes, they make for a lovely hollow on a windy day and the pasture is a home from home for the handful of cows that now graze where the men sweated and toiled.

In any farming community, in the last century, the production of lime dust was an important one, the lime used in mortar, the wash applied to many of the cottages and also added to the soil to help the potatoes grow. So the kiln would have been a busy place back then with the limestone being stored, burnt and then allowed to cool. It was a hot, hard, labour intensive process even before the prepared lime was put in sacks, stock-piled or sold and even then after all that, the kilns themselves had to be damped down before the workforce could go home.

But even then with the days work done and the men gone home, the kilns day were far from over. They still had one more vital service to provide. For it was then, with the huge ovens still giving off their heat on a cold winters night, that wanderers of the road, some might say tramps or hobo's, would sneak in through the gate and be able to warm themselves. Some might have even been able to cook a meal of scraps or left-overs, or if they were lucky, bacon and eggs that had been earned toiling in some farmers' field for the day. The kilns as they cooled were a special refuge and a rare respite for men who lived in the open air, but were not immune to the damp and the cold of a soft autumn night. The protective wall that separated the top of the kiln from the side road was the prime spot, making for a crude dormitory as it retained just enough heat to warm old bones long into the night.

This vestige of heat and maybe a bite of food was however a rare crumb of comfort in a hard life. But thinking back it's good to think that maybe sometimes it would have been just enough to remind these wanderers for a short while at least of better lives in better times. But just as surely as the heat from the kilns would fade it was never enough to take away the remorse and bitterness that went with past failures and lasting regrets. Their tales of fortunes, families and loves lost more than enough to fill many a volume but never written down, their stories forgotten and ignored just like the 'knights of the road' themselves. Their humble passage along the wild Kerry roads no more noticed than the passing of a shadow, or time itself.

Looking west from the top of the kiln, you can see the 'Druid's Circle', Kenmare's oldest monument and a good example of what religion meant in the days long before Saint Patrick and the mighty church of Rome. The circle is about 50 feet across and is set in a small meadow. It consists of fifteen standing stones that are only a few feet high, but weigh far more than any single man could lift. Standing in the centre is a 'Dolmen' or to be more precise a 'Cromlech', which is three stone uprights supporting a large cap-stone or ceremonial slab. Records suggest that it is probably at least four thousand years old.

The 'Druid's Circle' is without a doubt, the oldest monument in Kenmare and is very close to where the town's oldest inhabitants had once settled, on the banks of the 'Finnihy River'. These were 'The Beaker Folk', copper miners from the Iberian Peninsula in Spain, Holland and the Rhineland's who migrated to Ireland by way of France and England and ended up settling in the then relatively warm climate of South Kerry, which benefited greatly from the Gulf Stream. They were called 'The Beaker Folk' or 'Beaker People' because of their custom of burying beaker-shaped pottery alongside their dead together with a copper knife, a bow and flint-tipped arrows in rounded mounds or 'barrows', but individually, which was then an unusual custom.

The 'Beaker' people were at the forefront of the Bronze Age and became a focus of the widespread trade in gold and bronze ornaments. They were also in some way responsible for bringing the production of bronze to Ireland 4000 years ago. Importing tin from Cornwall and mining their own copper from mines in Allihies, West Cork. These two elements and their skill and experience producing one of the first sources of Bronze in Europe. It was probably the 'Beaker Folk' from Kerry and West Cork who opened up the trade routes to Wessex and other parts of Britain, eventually contributing to a Bronze industry in Britain that was to last for nearly 2000 years.

In Ireland 'The Beaker Folk' soon started to settle down and as they inter-married and integrated with the Irish, so began to lose something of their identity, language and customs. This was something that also happened in England, though some experts do believe that the remnants of the 'beaker' language still survive to this day as Welsh.

Throughout Ireland and the British Isles there are many 'Druid's Circles', the most well known being the late-Neolithic monument at Stonehenge, which though one of the finest examples of its kind in the world, is actually not a 'Druid's Circle' at all as the Druids never had anything whatsoever to do with the construction of this or any of the ancient monuments. The Druids were Celtic priests who had flourished in Britain at the time of the Roman conquest and did not build temples of their own .Stonehenge had been standing for about 2000 years and was most likely, already in ruins when they started to use it for rituals. Though the Stones, that had come all the way from the Preseli Mountains in South-west Wales, were not that important, as if a stone circle was not to hand, the druids could just as easily use a natural piece of rock or a clearing in the forest.

A great many stone circles, were built by the 'Beaker Folk' and they are also reputed to be responsible for the re-modelling of Stonehenge and the half circle of double bluestones in about 2100 BC.

The 'Beaker Folk' were a sophisticated people who made and used implements such as hammers, knives and chisels. They weaved in flax and linen and sowed their own barley, oats and rye. Though not a warlike people, they did make fine weapons and would use domesticated dogs for protecting their settlements. It is possible that the 'Beaker Folk' made their homes in the caves of Gortamullen, and were perhaps responsible for the Stone Circle on the banks of the Finnihy and not the Druid's at all. It is hard to be sure, some historians writing of the 'Beaker folk' in the Bronze Age claim that they were primitive cavemen who went around on all- fours and were not intelligent enough to farm or make tools. Others look at the evidence and recognise that the 'Beaker people' were an advanced race who were not only practical, innovative and ingenious, but were also very social people who made friends and not enemies wherever they went.

Stone Circles in Kerry are very numerous and there are a great many within a twenty mile radius of Kenmare, most requiring a bit of a trek to get to and often a little bit of negotiation as virtually all are on, or accessed through private land. Though this does not make them inaccessible, it does mean that most are in a natural, un-restored state and set in a field or halfway up a mountain give a true impression of how they are meant to look and indeed have looked for thousands of years.

Though Kenmare's 'Druid's circle' is on private land, it is considerably easier to get to than many ancient monuments and is, depending on your point of view, a nicely maintained historical beauty spot or a commercial tourist trap. Whatever your opinion, and whether you pay your entrance fee at the end of Market Street, or sneak in via the track beside the river, what it is and what it stands for is far more important than how it is perceived in the modern world, and the name by which it is known locally, as 'Bobby's Rocks'.

Kenmare has two churches, Protestant and Catholic respectively, their lofty spires rising up from opposite ends of the town. The Catholic church of The Holy Cross in Railway Road standing just a few yards from the main square and the protestant or Church Of Ireland's, St.Patricks on the Bridge Road just beyond the Post Office.

St. Patrick's at first glance is very reminiscent of a typically, English, rural Parish church and one that would not look out of place in any North Country village. Its setting, in an area sometimes known as 'Bell heights' might not seem as central as the catholic church with its proximity to the square. But being on the main road to Bantry or Glengarrif must afford some of its parishioners who live on the Ballygriffin side of the bridge an easier journey on most Sundays. St. Patrick's is also nicely placed for any English visitors staying at the Great Southern Hotel who can stroll to services in about five minutes.

The Catholic Church of the Holy Cross is of the grander, Irish style, built of sombre, grey stone and boasting a lofty spire that is part of the bell tower. The bell itself very much part of the fabric of Kenmare and a very real, reliable reminder to the people, that even as they toil and go about their business, any sense of responsibility or duty is still only part of a greater duty to a greater force than themselves. The bell rung by one of the town's most respected citizens three times a day, without fail, come hail, rain or shine at seven o'clock in the morning, twelve noon and six in the evening at a time referred to since medieval times as 'The Angelus'.

But the bell ringer was more than just a human chronometer. It was also his job to announce. The melancholy tones of the great bell an apt and fitting accompaniment for the last journey of the departed. The whole valley echoing with its soft tones as old friends and relatives paid their last respects and even total strangers in the town might pause to make the sign of the cross and pray a few words.

The Kenmare bell is not just a reminder of past times when it would signify the start of the day's toil, dinner time, mass or the end of the working day. The tolling of the bell was and still is a re-assurance of normality that all is well and as you watch shoppers pause in the midday heat to make the sign of the cross, you can't help but feel that

44

this how God and the parish priest would want it to be. For faith to be a part of your every day and not just a few hours on Sunday. The great bell not just a timepiece for the poor folk, who had no clocks or watches, or the equivalent of the klaxon at the end of the shift, but a constant, reliable, dependable testament to a greater power and a sound that might honestly be called the heartbeat of Kenmare.

The church's interior is no less imposing and boasts one of the most impressive Stone and marble altars in all Kerry with three Stations of the Cross carved magnificently into the frontispiece. The two side altars are no less splendid and showcase the work of talented Irish craftsmen who's depiction of the 'Madonna and Child' and the 'Crucifixion' are as faultless as the stone that almost comes alive in the early evening sunlight filtering through the stained glass like a giant magic lantern slide.

The beauty of Holy Cross is due to the munificence of the 3rd Marquis of Lansdowne and other wealthy benefactors. Father John O'Sullivan was responsible for the building of the church and for his labours now lays at rest under 'Our Lady's altar. That he did a fine job made plain at his funeral, when the Bishop of Kerry called Holy Cross, 'The loveliest Ornament of the Diocese'.

The site of the church and the land around it was also given by the 3rd Marquis. The Lansdowne family had acquired pretty much all the land around Kenmare by 'right of Conquest'. Before Holy Cross was built the main place of worship was a chapel built in1799 in Shelbourne Street. Though nothing of the structure remains, if you look the site can still be seen, set back from the road, to the left of the Great Southern Hotel entrance and to the rear of the 'Munster and Leinster' bank, that is now the private residence of a local doctor.

At the east end of 'Our Lady's Bridge' is a much clustered sign post and on one arm that points along the coast road to the 'Beara Peninsula' is a sign for 'Derreen House and Gardens.

Set on a promontory overlooking Killmakilloge Harbour, 'Derreen House' is the family home of the Lansdowne family .Its first owner and builder was Peter McSweeney, a man who had been a direct descendant of the old chiefs of Berehaven and who ruled his land like a drunken despot. Constantly at war with his tenants and neighbours he was only too happy to settle disputes in the law courts or in the fields and was reputed to have shot two men in separate duels before litigation and eventually the famine crippled his fortune. The house and lands then passed to the Lansdowne family and became home to John Petty-Fitzmaurice the 1st Marquis of Lansdowne (1737-1805) and thereafter the main residence for his forebears. Though initially the land around the house suffered the same fate as any other piece of woodland under Petty's domain and was cut down for fuel for the iron furnaces and remained scarred for many years after, it did not remain so and taking full advantage of the warm comforts of the Gulf Stream the gardens, which cover 60 acres, were extensively landscaped in 1873. It was an ambitious project and though many of the trees and shrubs came from the tropics most seemed to flourish in Kerry's temperate climate. The huge, New Zealand tree fern which resembles a palm set atop a tree trunk, did especially well and was able to maintain its customary height of 16 to 30 feet, with leaves measuring ten feet in length. Making it the largest *'crystomeria elegans'* in all Ireland.

The team of full-time gardeners saw many well known visitors enjoying the fruits of their labours. One in particular was the English Historian, James Anthony Froude who resided at the house in 1867. Amongst his famous works was 'The history of England from the fall of Wolsley to the defeat of the Spanish Armada'. The work, which ran to twelve volumes, took him fourteen years to complete. He was appointed Regis Professor of Modern History at Oxford in 1892 when he was 76 years of age and he died in Oxford on October 20th 1894.

Like many fine mansions in Kerry, Derreen House was burnt down during the 'Troubles' of 1921-22, but was rebuilt and is still a fine stop-off on the tourist trail and an ideal place to spend a couple of hours enjoying the magnificent gardens after the 16 mile drive from Kenmare.

If you continue along the coast road, there is a lovely clear view of the Kenmare Bay at Dawros, but little else, just a few houses, a National school and a small Catholic Church nestling amongst the pines. Across the bay there at least twenty Islands, mostly small and uninhabited, unlike Dinish Island which has been the much envied home for various families over the years and still must boast some of the finest views from any private house on the Kenmare River.

Five miles on from peaceful Dawros you take a left turn onto a 'green' or unmade road that winds its way through the Cloonee and Inchequin Loughs, which are well known to any keen anglers for their fine stock of trout and help to drain the rain from the Caha Mountains. At the end of the road is the 'Ishachbuderlick Waterfall', which is better known as Gleninchiquin.

Thirteen hundred feet above Lough Inchequin six, separate mountain streams form a small lake called 'Cummeenaloghann'and from this lake the waterfall spills over the mountain side to fall six hundred feet. From a distance the waterfall gives the appearance of a white, vein of marble, or when the waters are in full flood, it has been compared to a careless can of white paint left to spill on the dark rock. It is a unique spectacle and up close the spray creates a rainbow that is the ideal advert for peace and solitude, and all free, designed and built by Mother Nature and regularly serviced by God's soft rain.

Back on the main road, you soon come to a junction where, in the reign of Queen Victoria, a Royal Irish constabulary barracks sat. From here, both roads lead to Lauragh, one around 'Knockanouganish Mountain' and the other through Lehid wood. A interesting route that is more scenic and brings you out past a small quay, a public house and then facing you 'Killmakilloge Harbour'.

It is a fine view and a few years ago, much to the disgust of the local inhabitants, someone decided to dump four rusting salvage vessels by the dog-legged quay, their intrusion on the view almost as bad as the risk they pose to curious children who might see the hulks as a playground. We can only hope that at some point soon they will be taken away before anyone is hurt.

Facing the old harbour wall where many a harvest has been loaded at the quayside is Mr. Teddy O'Sullivan's bar and shop, not as you might expect two separate premises, but in fact just the one unique, very Irish, establishment where the wife could do the shopping catch up on the local news and keep an eye on the husband who was partaking of something damp to quell the thirst.

Lauragh is well sheltered from the Atlantic squalls by plenty of mature Pine trees, though it's not what you might call a town, but more of a district like its neighbour, nearby Tuosist. Just a church, a Post Office and a National School that is only open in the summer for foreign students, and of course. Some might say the most important local amenity, the public house. Like many rural pubs, there are no fitted carpets or lounge seats, just a simple, traditional interior and an old wringer/mangle standing, redundant in one corner to perhaps remind the drinkers that their hard day in the fields was not the only labour to be endured on a work day?

A couple of miles further, and on a road that goes to the head of the Glanmore Valley, stands a deserted forge with the classic horse-shoe shaped doorway that was a symbol of the blacksmiths trade, and an advertisement for all the skills he would offer the local community. The road is steep and dramatic, the Mountains with names as beautiful as their very peaks; Foileman, Curraghreaglia, Lackabane, Tooth, Knockastumpa, Stookeennalackareha and many many more. Each one more rugged, more jagged, more steep, more wild than its counterpart, a romantic wilderness that would look more at home in the wilds of Canada than the borders of Cork and Kerry.

Below splashed across the valley is Glanmore lake, and upon its calm surface a small island stands in the shadows of the surrounding mountains. On the island, almost hidden in the trees lays the ruins of an old house that must have been the perfect haven for someone who loved loneliness and peace of mind. The ideal residence for an author, a poet or a landscape painter. Either profession suiting the seclusion, the quiet and the beauty. Never mind the utter inspiration of the mountains and the dramatic views that are visible from the Healy Pass at the head of the valley.

Some of the houses and cottages in and around Lauragh and the Glanmore Valley are very much of the 'English' style. This is because many were built by Lord Henry Petty as tied houses for his tenants and workers. One particularly fine example being 'Glanmore School' with its attic bedrooms and quaint gables, which is now a popular Youth Hostel in a perfect setting.

Towards the east, at the head of the Glanmore Valley is the 'Healy Pass' 1081 feet above sea level and the boundary line between County Cork and county Kerry. This high point marked with a fine white marble statue of Christ at Calvary that looks down on a road that is reputed to have more hair-pin bends than any other road in Ireland. It was completed in 1932 after being built on and off for over 85 years. Began as a Famine relief project during the Great Famine of 1845-1859, and started at each end simultaneously, Lauragh Bridge in the west and Adrigole in the east, work was constantly delayed by the terrible circumstances and many men and women actually died in the construction. Some might say far too high a price for the meagre eight pennies a day wages. Even as recently as 1903 the stretch of road from Clogherane Bridge to the slopes of Ballagscart Mountain was yet to be completed. Given the cost in time, effort and lives the highway is more memorial than mere road and a credit to the men who literally climbed a mountain to complete this impressive task.

On the Kerry side of the pass, a signpost stands near the Mourin Bridge spanning the Owenshagh River. Upon it two arrows point to Kenmare, one saying 15 miles and one saying 17. The longest route is the coast road that takes you the long way to Lehid harbour and Tuosist. The other, the mountain route between Knockanouganish and Knockgarriff that brings you out by the Old constabulary Barracks that stand as a reminder of the 1921-1922 troubles. All of this beautiful scenery, stretching from Lauragh to beyond Kenmare was owned by the Lansdowne family. Most acquired by William Petty in the times before Ireland became a republic. Back then much of Ireland was owned by English Landlords who could become very wealthy from the crops, which given the ideal soil and climate, were often substantial. In 1870, the Lansdowne estate alone had some 121,349 statute acres with a yield of £33, 342 just in rents alone. (In 1970, that same figure would be more like £500,000.)

Many of the English landlords hardly ever saw their estates in Ireland, of course for many of them this was not so surprising as with larger estates in England to look after Irish land was perhaps not deemed as important, and wasn't given the attention that it needed. This could cause problems for the Irish tenant farmers and the label applied to their English Masters as 'Absent Landlords was not a complimentary one.

The 3rd Marquis of Lansdowne was no different, he left the running of his Irish estate to a Mr.William Trench and divided most of his time between his English estate at 'Bowood' near Calne in Wiltshire, his London residence in Berkeley Square or France. Where, such was the status of the Marquis that he would often attend house parties at the 'Chateau de Compeigne' in Northern France that were hosted by the Empress Eugenie and her husband Napoleon III. Such parties would commence at 7.00pm after a days hunting, 120 guests entertained to a lavish banquet in grand style and grand company. It was not uncommon for the Marquis to share a table with both the ruler of France and the future king of England, then known as Edward Prince of Wales.

In London it was the 3rd Marquis that did the entertaining and amongst many leading intellectuals and politicians of the day, he was known to be especially fond of the beloved Irish poet Thomas Moore 1779-1852.

Thomas Moore had studied at Trinity College in Dublin, then at the age of twenty came to London to enter the Middle Temple, one of the Inns of Court. Here he became a protégé of Lord Moira and was appointed Secretary of the Admiralty in Bermuda. But he quickly became bored and returned to England to find that his deputy in Bermuda had embezzled money from the Admiralty and because Moore was in charge, he was also responsible. Though he did pay the money back it was only with the kind assistance of Lord Henry.

Not just a renowned poet, Thomas was also a fine musician and after his book of 'Irish Melodies' was published he quickly became very popular in his native Ireland, though his poems first appeared under the pseudonym of 'Thomas Little'.

By September 1817 Thomas had married Bessie Dyke who at 16 was a young mother and their first two children died in their infancy. Shortly after the death of their second daughter Barbara, and with Just Anastasia as an heir, Lord Lansdowne offered Thomas and Betsy a lovely house with beautiful gardens in Broham. The house was called 'Sloperton Cottage, a stunning 18th Century residence just 4 miles from the Marquis' Estate at Bowood. Thomas gladly accepted and enjoyed both the low rent and the proximity to Lord Henry. He was a regular visitor to Bowood and attended many dinner parties though Bessie would always excuse herself and never attended.

The happy couple were also blessed with two sons, Tom and Russell but then tragedy struck and Anastasia developed consumption and died in the spring of 1829. It was something Thomas never got over and when Russell and then Tom died, he was heartbroken. Two years later he suffered a severe stroke, became helpless and confused and passed away on February 20th 1852. He was buried in Broham graveyard with his beloved Anastasia. Bessie lived on for another 13 years, until she too joined her husband in eternal rest.

It's strange to think that had circumstances been different, instead of Sloperton, the Marquis might well have rented the couple Derreen House and perhaps life could have been less tragic for this great Irish poet and musician.

> *Oh! Blame not the bard, if he fly to the bowers,*
> *Where pleasure lies carelessly smiling at fame;*
> *He was born for much more, and in happier hours,*
> *His soul might have burn'd with a holier flame.*

-Thomas Moore.

CHAPTER FOUR.

There were many arguments between the Marquis' agent William Trench and the Parish priest Father O'Sullivan. One in particular was over the site of the Holy Cross Church, for though the land was freely given by the 3rd Marquis, Trench had never reached any formal agreement over the actual siting of the Church as was his responsibility as Land Agent and Lord Lansdowne's official representative and when Father O'Sullivan went over Trench's head and agreed a site with the Marquis himself, the Agent was not especially pleased.

The parish priest, who felt that he had got one over on the Agent, was alleged to have told Trench, *'That I will crow over you yet!'* Though some people say it was just an offhand remark or perhaps even a tall tale. When you then realise that atop the weathervane on the spire of Holy Cross, stands a cock, and that a cock is indeed a rare sight on top of any weathervane on any Catholic Church, you start to wonder if Father O'Sullivan really got to make his point after all. For if there was no substance in the story, why did a much aggrieved William Trench have the window of his estate office that overlooked the spire 'filled in'?

When you view the office, a well-constructed, grey-stone, one-storey building, that is still standing rather isolated in a small, green pasture set back from the square and still very much in the shadow of the Church spire. You can't help but feel that it was the Parish Priest that had the last word, the spire like a stern teacher standing over a naughty pupil with a beckoning finger. Could there be better proof of Father O'Sullivans prophecy?

Father O'Sullivan served the parish of Kenmare well for 35 years. A true Kerryman born in the town of Tralee, he became Parish Priest in 1839 and was keen to encourage the education of all children. To achieve this Father John had brought the 'Presentation Sisters' from their convent in CastleIsland to Kenmare. They founded a new convent in 1859 and though their teaching was very successful a bit of a dispute arose with Father John when he tried to give the good sisters an extra hour's rest in the morning. His idea being that because school did not commence until 10.00a.m, the sisters could have a rest and rise at 6.00.am instead of the usual 5.00.a.m start to the day.

But because of their strict religious orders, the Sisters could not agree and feeling somewhat affronted by what they failed to see as a misplaced act of kindness they returned to their Convent in CastleIsland. It was a great shame, the Board of Education had already failed in their attempt to set up industrial schools in Kerry between 1850 and 1854 and so with the Presentation Sisters gone, there was once again no school in Kenmare.

But such are the twists and turns of fate that in the same year that the Presentation Sisters departed in 1861, a certain Mother O'Hagan and three other sisters came to the town and realising a need, founded the 'Poor Clare's Convent at Kenmare.' They had travelled from the 'Poor Clare's' Convent in Newry, on the borders of Counties Down and Armagh, arriving in the then, quiet, country town after a very long and arduous journey by road. It was to be another two years before the Dublin - Killarney railway was completed in 1863 and words like travel and comfort were unlikely to be used in the same sentence. Not un-used to hardship, until a part of their convent was finished, the sisters had to endure the harsh Kerry winter of rain and cold winds in 'Rose Cottage' which still stands only a few hundred yards from the convent gates at the North West corner of the square. At that time there was no still no water supply, the only light came from tallow candles and the only heat was that of the open-hearth fire.

Though this life was no more 'bare and humble' than convent life in Newry it was infinitely preferable to the abject poverty that many local people lived in. For them home was the 'Byre' type of mud cabin that was commonplace throughout all Ireland at the end of the 19th Century and with the harsh, Spartan dwelling came poverty, hunger and disease. These appalling conditions were to have a profound effect upon one of the Poor Clare's nuns. Her name was Sister Mary Francis Clare and she'd been born in Coolock in 1828 about three miles from Dublin city. She came from an Anglo-Irish Protestant family and had been a sister in the church of England before converting to Catholicism and entering the 'Poor Clare's' on the 2nd of July 1859. A year and a day later, by special concession she took her final vows and became Sister Mary Francis.

It wasn't long before she was on the move south to Kerry. She described her journey through Killarney while the nuns rested for a while at the Bishop of Kerry's palace near St.Mary's. Giving a true inkling of where her true feelings lay when she described it as 'a magnificent building, but a strange contrast to the misery, dirt and wretchedness around'. She also recorded, 'how she never knew what poverty was until she went to Kerry. Nothing she encountered in the slums of the east end of London were so terrible, so squalid or so sad as the plight of the poor wretches she had come amongst'.

A true philanthropist, Sister Mary was always keen to get involved with any debate that touched on the poverty she saw around her and the causes such as unemployment and even famine which was always a very real threat every harvest and one that could ultimately lead to hunger and even starvation.

But of all the problems she saw on her regular forays beyond the closed convent doors, one in particular seemed to be at the heart of so many social ills. The case of the Absentee Landlords and there were many in, or to be more correct, out of Ireland. Rich men who regarded their 'Irish estates' as secondary holdings in terms of importance, and the tenant farmers and their families as of slightly less worth than the cattle and sheep they tended. Indeed during the 1870's the dirt-poor Kerry farmers were worse off than slaves, as Sister Mary wrote; 'in Ireland, it quite depends on the will of the proprietor, whether he lets his lands to his tenants, which will enable them to feed their families on the coarsest food, and to clothe them in the coarsest raiment's if a famine occurs. And in some parts of Ireland famines are of annual occurrence, the landlord is not obliged to do anything for his tenant, but the tenant must pay his rent!'

This brutal style of estate management made any problems worse, and with the cold, 'at arms length' overseeing of matters through a land agent with little real power everything naturally took longer to be dealt with, usually resulting in the small problems turning into big ones and serious issues such as poverty ignored or allowed to quickly spiral out of control. Not that the absentee Landlord actually gave a damn in his palatial English estate, to him the Irish were no different to any tenant, always complaining about something. But because they were so faraway he usually tended not to listen, never mind care.

Sister Mary quickly became a driving force in the world of social reform and her indomitable spirit made her one of the best known personalities of her time and in Kenmare and Kerry one of the most influential.

It was probably through her overwhelming desire to allow women to be educated on a similar footing to men that she came up with one of her most innovative and lasting ideas. That of teaching the local girls the art of lace making, not just as 'women's work' or simply something to do, but as a genuine, valued skill and one that quickly became not just a thriving cottage industry, but something that would eventually became synonymous with Kenmare itself.

Many years later 'Point Lace' from the Kenmare Convent won first place in the 'South Kensington' competition of 1886 and in 1893 did very well at the 'Chicago World's fair'. The lace is still highly prized and some prime examples are reputed to be worth their weight in gold. It is able to be seen, on occasion, by visitors to the convent as the order of the 'Poor Clare's' was dispensed with as a closed order by Pope John the 23rd and the gates to it and the adjacent churchyard are now open to all.

Not content with all her good works, Sister Mary then went on to set up the Famine Relief Fund in 1879 with the Protestant Rector of St.Patricks, the Reverend George McCutchan who came from Limerick and Mr. Michael Cronin who became secretary.

Famine was a constant threat to the poor who relied almost exclusively on a diet of potatoes. With an average adult able to consume up to 10lb's of potatoes a day, this meant that the country needed to produce at least 15 million tons per year. 47% of this went for human consumption, 33% as animal feed, 13% for seed, 5% as waste and only 2% for export. It was a recipe for disaster as all other crops produced in Ireland, including those produced in times of dire need were exported to England, leaving the poor with no alternative other than starvation

There were serious famines in Ireland in 1741 when 300,000 people died, further catastrophes in 1817 and 1821 and in 1845-46 the great Famine struck. It was a time when

5 million out of a total population of only 8 million, were totally dependant on the potato crop that was rotting in the ground. It and the famines that occurred thereafter showed in graphic terms how vulnerable the poor were in Ireland, as meat was still considered a luxury and ignorance rendered humble crops such as cabbage to be deemed only secondary and never as worthy as the mighty spud, which when combined with some dairy produce, other vegetables and fish made for a healthy, well balanced diet. It was in fact the case, that for many years the dirt poor Irish were at least healthier than many of their European counterparts who considered bread the superior food source.

Sister Mary's fund was able to raise £15, 000 which was a huge sum in those days, equivalent to about half a million in today's money. But besides the distribution of money and food, there was also the more valuable provision of seed potatoes for next year. An element of Famine relief that showed a true understanding of the problems faced by the poor and one that went beyond the 'hand-out' policy which solved today's problem but didn't stop the same thing from happening tomorrow.

The Famine relief fund was years ahead of its time and a classic example of 'Church Unity' at a time when many in the upper echelons of both protestant and catholic churches would have frowned on such collaboration. There were certainly some people locally who had their ethical doubts about a Catholic nun and a Protestant rector providing the greatest charity of all and literally saving the lives of a great many men, women and children. But for a time religious differences, if there were in fact any, were ignored and when upwards of 500 people assembled in the town square for the distribution of food and seed potatoes, the true meaning of Christian charity was there for all to see.

In the 19th Century, Famine in Ireland was a more frequent occurrence than elsewhere in Europe and more devastating because of the people's dependence on the potato and the abject poverty in which they lived. Prior to 1845 famine would occur if any potato crop failed, but because these events were usually localised and there was a sound system of state relief, the effect could be seriously minimised without extensive loss of life. But the blight that struck in 1845 was something new, a much more virulent disease that quickly spread from the eastern seaboard of the United States to southern France, Switzerland, Eastern Germany and Ireland, where a damp, sunless summer compounded the effect.

For the dirt-poor, tenant farmers who utterly relied upon the potato crop it was a devastating experience, their fortunes literally changing overnight as a polluting fungus infected the rich, green foliage of the healthy plant and it quickly became this black, putrid mass of rotting tubers. The stench of the lost harvest like the smell of death itself, as with little in the way of alternatives, the loss of the potato crop was as good as a death sentence for the farmer and his family.

With reports claiming that between three quarters and nine tenths of the potato crop had been lost, those that were left were quickly consumed and food prices rocketed. Since most other foods were beyond the reach of the poor in normal circumstances and the British government were reluctant to divert exports of corn, there were few options for the starving. One possible substitute during these terrible circumstances was 'Indian Maize'; this was imported from America, but proved a poor substitute in many ways. Its biggest problem was that it had to be cooked and the people who were already weak from hunger had no strength to collect turf from the store sheds, never mind cut it from the bogs. This meant that there was no fuel for the fire, and no fire meant that the maize couldn't be cooked and had to be eaten raw by the starving people. Which made it unpalatable and of little dietary benefit.

As if starvation wasn't bad enough, the people who were already weak, hungry, weary and unable to help themselves also lived under the constant threat of eviction. Their Landlords caring little for the plight of their tenants when rent was due, starving families literally put out of their homes, then having to watch as the 'Byre' was rendered inhospitable by the Lord's henchmen who would split the front door, tumble the roof and even demolish walls so as to leave no shelter from the elements. Families literally forced to live in ditches at the side of the road or anywhere else that some shelter could be had from the often malevolent weather.

They were cruel times to be poor and starving, but to be homeless? To be deprived of even the most basic shelter from the fierce weather was an act of inhuman barbarity. But sadly it was only too common and other Landlords were even more ruthless Lord Kinston owner of the Barony of Fermoy did not just forcibly evict thousands of wretched individuals from their homes in Fermoy, Ballyhooly, Mallow, Kildorrey, Charleville and Kilworth. Using his power as Magistrate he would not hesitate to transport five hundred people at a time to far off Quebec, many who were never to return to their homeland. Other architects of this misery and injustice were Lord Mount Cashel of Kilworth, Lord Doveraile and Lord Ennismore. In 1846 alone, over 32,000 unfortunate victims were landed in Quebec and Montreal, followed by another 70,000 in 1847. Lord Kingston shifting 1,600 people in one consignment, while his conspirators were responsible for upwards of 2000 human beings being transported from their estates for the wretched crime of poverty. Largely overlooked and ignored by many, these acts were comparable to the forced transportation of over

50,000 men, women and children to Barbados and Virginia in the 1650's.

Though there were some that sought to justify the famine as an act of God on a par with any biblical tale of suffering, it was a cruel act of nature that was compounded by circumstances and ultimately exploited by unscrupulous landlords who used the non-payment of rent by starving, impoverished souls as an excuse to clear their lands for more profitable uses. That the famine should have happened at all was a calamity, that it should have been made worse by man's greed and intolerance to their own kind was a travesty and the fact that rebellion and revolt was to follow such acts, was not a coincidence.

But for those that escaped hunger, eviction and enforced transportation, life was not much better. In the 19th Century a family did what ever it could to make a little money and it was still very much the custom in many area's for a father to put a daughter into service; this could be in a large house or mansion, the big houses of the middle class, local presbyteries and even large public bars. Apart from long hours, hard work and a diet of weak tea and dry bread, it was not uncommon for the poor girl to receive no wages, as they would be handed straight over to her father to support the rest of the family. For many it was no different to slave labour, but in spite of the hardship and bad treatment of many employers they could not give up their job as to do so would invariably lose the family money and cause their siblings greater suffering and even result in destitution. Even on the farms, a young girl that was born on a farm would usually end up having to give her life to that farm and probably in the process be no better thought of than the cattle or sheep. That any child, never mind a daughter might attend school was for many not even a remote possibility.

Father John O'Sullivan was a much liked Parish Priest and always had only the very best of intentions for both Church and Town and would do what he thought to be right even if it brought him into dispute with the local people. Though of great benefit for the town, his bringing of the Presentation Sisters to Kenmare had angered the Marquis' land agent William Trench and caused on-going friction that was to continue for many years. Also his handling of the 'timetable' matter that led to the Presentation Sisters departure had been seen by some locals as a slighting of the Sisters' good name and not the simple misunderstanding it had in fact been.

Whatever the good Father's standing in the town, he must have been relieved then when the 'Poor Clare's and Mother O'Hagan established the convent school in the town.

Mother O'Hagan it should be noted was none other than the sister of Thomas O'Hagan the then Chancellor of the Exchequer under William Gladstone, a man of some standing who went on to become the first Catholic Lord Chancellor of Ireland in 1870.

Somewhat against popular thinking of the time, Father O'Sullivan had always set great store in the provision of education and he was very gratified by the work of Mother O'Hagan and her hardworking colleague Sister Mary Francis who while still trying to deal with the aftermath of the Famine was greatly distressed by the fact that in the Caherciveen area alone there were some 500 children unfit to appear in school. In a poor country that was very much still in recovery mode, Education was perhaps not deemed as worthy a cause as alleviating hunger and poverty and Sister Mary Francis certainly had her work cut out for a number of years. But even with set-backs like these by 1860 there were 1,500 schools in Munster and all but a very few children were not receiving some form of learning, so the good Sisters work was not without its rewards.

But unfortunately there were some that were not so in favour of her hard work, the ecclesiastical Authorities in particular seeming to take a dim view if her habits of fraternising with the enemy and working with Rector McCutchan of the Protestant Church on famine relief projects. Even though she had received Papal congratulations from Pope Pius IX in 1870 for her relief fund work there were many in the Church that didn't care for this attitude of 'rocking the boat' or even the 'biting of the hand that feeds,' when she took absentee landlords to task over their poor treatment of their tenants and their reluctance to grant any rights whatsoever to men and women who had by their birthright a justified claim to the soil they worked.

Her books too created quite a stir, especially her autobiography 'The Nun of Kenmare' which became a major source of income for the Convent. Her writings voicing her support for 'The Land league' and giving vent to her disputes with the Lansdowne estate Landlords and even Dr.David Moriarty, the Bishop of Kerry.

Sister Mary's other great gift to Kenmare, the lace making, was to add a coincidental twist when ten years later she was to found an order of 'The Sisters of Saint Joseph of Peace' in Nottingham an English Town that is also noted for its lace-making.

At the time of writing there is an enormous amount of interest in the plan to bring Sister Mary Francis' remains back to Kenmare, a place she loved and was in turn much beloved in by the poor, the starving and the homeless. A true philanthropist who recognised the need for practical sustenance for the body as well as the soul, she was not afraid to voice her opinions, stand by her principals and do 'God's work' in a way that ensures her respect and devotion in Kenmare to this day. That respect and memory still remaining in the hearts of the older generations whose forebears probably owe a great deal to 'The Nun of Kenmare'.

Kenmare's lace making soon became a successful cottage industry with the girls who worked in the industrial school within the convent building able to earn between five and eighteen shillings a week in 1864. The rate of pay depended on their age and how skilled they were. Though it seems meagre, when you think that Lace makers in Nottingham in England were paid three shillings and four pence a day and eventually had to go on strike in 1874 to get a raise to four shillings, they were not so hard done by and given the lower cost of living in Ireland at the time, were in real terms probably a little bit better off. Lace making was and indeed still is a highly skilled profession requiring great patience and dexterity and in a 19th Century that was to all intents and purposes a 'man's world', a rare industry where women held sway and still do.

Then in the autumn of 1880 Sister Mary Francis received a letter from London that was to change her life. A vicious death threat reminding her and the people around her that, even though she had saved many, many lives and improved the lot of countless others, she still had her enemies and regardless of her good name and reputation was very vulnerable to the pressure that these enemies could bring to bear. Especially when they were influential public figures.

One such man was Charles Russell Q.C and M.P, later to become Lord Russell of Killowen, a member of the Royal Agriculture Commission. Who by launching an investigation caused Sister Mary Francis' Relief fund to be closed in 1880. Summoned to appear before the commission, she was questioned on her views on absentee Landlords, and had to suffer the ignominy of listening to Kenmare's new parish priest, Archdeacon Higgins saying that; 'He knew the 3rd Marquis to be the best Landlord in all Kerry, if not all Ireland.' Something of a contradiction to an article in the 'Cork Examiner' on the 22nd of November that quoted; 'how grievances of high rents on the Lansdowne estate existed for twenty years and had remained un-addressed.'

But it was a losing battle and though Sister Mary Francis was much comforted by a visit to the 'Poor Clare's 'Convent by the Poet Laureate, Alfred Lord Tennyson in December 1880, that brought her great kindness and peace of mind. Her time in Kerry was almost at an end, and on 16th November 1881, with much regret, sorrow and very much against her will. Sister Mary Francis was transferred back to the Convent at Newry, accompanied by her secretary Miss Downing and Father Maurice Neligan.

Back in Kenmare Father O'Sullivan's replacement, the politically astute, Archdeacon Higgins who came from nearby Killarney had been moved to Tralee and a new Father O'Sullivan came to Kenmare from nearby Cahir. Father Michael was about as local as you could get, a great believer in home rule, the rights of tenants and an avid supporter of Sister Mary Francis. Who, though in exile in Newry wrote in her book 'Case for Ireland' in 1881, of the suffering of tenants and the cruel system of landlords. But Archdeacon Higgins, who was by now Bishop of Kerry, not only prevented all publication of her works, but made sure that the Famine Relief Fund stayed closed as well. And with Sister Mary Francis gagged and her good works curtailed it seemed that the suffering of the poor and the impoverished would go on.

But Sister Mary was not to be silent or inactive. Whilst on their journey from Kenmare to Newry, their party had stopped at Knock in county Mayo and the good sister had once more seen the potential for her good works, and so with the help of Archbishop McEvilly managed to obtain a transfer from Kenmare to Knock. No mean feat considering her fall from grace.

But if she thought establishing a convent in Knock was to be easy, she was sadly mistaken and had to wait eight months before the Archbishop of Tuam granted her permission to start work on the building of a convent. Even then she was badly treated by her superiors and with no postulants and a lay sister who could not read or write was forced to live in a stable where she contracted diphtheria, before finally getting two rooms in a public house.

Archdeacon Cavanagh, the Parish Priest of Knock was very much in favour of Sister Mary founding a new order, and supported her as over the next two years she opened two schools. One, an industrial school on similar lines to Kenmare and the other an ordinary school where she was eventually joined by another lay sister and six young women who became novices. Though Sister Mary worked tirelessly to encourage education for all and equal rights for women, she was a woman in a man's world and it was always men in high places that went against her, thus the Archbishop of Tuam never gave his approval for her good works and without it, and feeling that her task was an uphill struggle, Sister Mary Francis became very discouraged and feeling humiliated and let down, left Knock on the 1st of November 1883 with the faithful Miss Downing.

Then 55 years of age and both disillusioned and broken hearted to see twenty years of good works gone, Sister Mary Francis left Ireland in and went to live in Grimsby in England. Here with Miss Downing and four novices, she lived a very different life on the east coast of Lincolnshire, at the mouth of the Humber. The six women receiving more warmth from the bracing east winds than they ever had from the Archbishop of Tuam.

Here they were made the first 'Sisters of Saint Joseph

of Peace' in Nottingham Cathedral on the 7th January 1884, by the Bishop of Nottingham, Edward Bagshawe. Sister Mary spent a while in Nottingham, and then in February received a private audience with Pope Leo XIII. Arriving back in England with the idea of founding a religious house in the Bishop's diocese. It was approved by both Bishop and Pope.

Then when most people her age would have been thinking about settling down, she set sail for America to raise funds for a campaign intent on building homes for working class girls who were still being exploited by both family and employers. But even with a strong, Irish influence, she met worse opposition than she had in Ireland.

Cardinal Mcloskey forbade Sister Mary from even entering New York and the Church Hierarchy in Chicago and Baltimore refused to help at all. Everywhere she went it was the same story and after many illnesses and even two operations in 1892 and 1893 she was forced to leave America and return to England with one condition that has no cure, a broken heart.

Bitterly disappointed that her cause had been frustrated by narrow-minded, male bigots who resented that she was a woman even more than they despised her concern for others. She left the Catholic Church to become a Methodist and lived out the rest of her life like an exile in England where she died aged 71 on the 5th of June 1899 and was buried in an Anglican churchyard in Leamington Spa Warwickshire.

During her life Sister Mary wrote many excellent reference books; 'An Illustrated History of Ireland from the Earliest Period. 'The Life of Saint Patrick. Apostle of Ireland 1870.' But she will probably be best remembered for her autobiography, 'The Nun of Kenmare', that she wrote in 1895.

In a long life she did many good works for many people. Though she did manage to make a name for herself and also carved out a worthy reputation that some might say went against the vows of humility and piety, she only ever used it for common good. Using it to encourage Church unity, to set up Famine relief funds, Industrial Schools, convents and normal schools. She also met the great and the good, from Popes to Poets, visited many places and many countries but it's reasonable to think that in spite of all the travelling that was to become a feature of the latter years, perhaps it was a little market town in Kerry that she would often think of. A town that always held a special place in her heart. A town where she made the biggest differences to ordinary people's lives, a town where her legacy of Protestant and Catholic unity still lives on a hundred years later. A town she thought to include in the title of the story of her life and perhaps a town she thought of as her home, Kenmare.

CHAPTER FIVE.
The Fair Day - 'Cean Mara' - Passenger Cars

The most important day in Kenmare's calendar, apart from Christmas and Easter, is the 15th of August, celebrated by the town and country folks alike as a holiday, but more importantly known as the Fair Day.

In the Church calendar it is the feast of the Assumption and for many, the day begins with Mass, the aisles swelled with farmers with dirty boots and hedgerow switches showing their respect, and maybe even trying to curry favour with the big man, before heading back into Main Street or the Square for the other main business of the day. The cut and thrust of cattle trading.

Any Fair day in Ireland means the same thing, cattle, sheep and horse sales the top of a long list that can also include chickens, ducks, cats, donkeys, pigs, dogs, turf, straw, vegetables, tools, boots, clothes and any number of other things that are indispensable to the lives of the farmers who throng the town from dawn to dusk. Their animals tethered to lamp posts and railings or herded quietly by the kerbs, there are no stalls or pens, or designated areas for livestock and so the cars and trucks and trailers have to vie for space with horses and bullocks and ewes. The animals patiently waiting as if they understood the long, delicate negotiations that are taking place amongst serious men with weather-worn caps and wind-burned faces. Any unrest amongst the four-legged ranks quickly and efficiently dispelled with a whistle, a yell or a stinging stick.

At times, as you watch the hard-earned cash changing hands and the deals being struck over a nod and a handshake, it could be any year in the last fifty, the farmers' faces and severe black suits showing the wear and tear of hard lives at the mercy of the elements. Main street and the Square looking just as they must have been before the coming of the motor car, when livestock had to be got to town on foot, often travelling through the night so as to be in ready at the crack of dawn and the commencement of trading. Cattle, sheep and horses thronging the narrow roads and lanes, while only the pigs and crated hens got to travel in the relative style of the donkey and cart with the farmer and his family.

Though a public holiday for the townspeople and something of an attraction for tourists who flock to see the animals and soak up the atmosphere. For the farmers its an important working day and the flocks of mountain sheep nibbling at the cobbles in Market Street, or the Heifers grazing at the entrance to the Great Southern hotel are not just quaint curiosities or rare photo opportunity's. They are business opportunities and could represent a significant chunk of the farm's income for the next twelve months. The money to be made on the 15[th of] August could make a big difference come the 15th of December, and there is an earnest concentration in the faces of even the children selling chickens or prized puppies, knowing as they do that this is as much their living, as it is their Mothers and Fathers.

Though still a special day in the Town's Calendar and an important one for all concerned, it has to be said that the Fair Day has declined somewhat over the years and not just in the sheer numbers of animals on the streets. Though still an impressive spectacle for tourists and 'townies', for the locals it must seem at time to be little more than a shadow of its former self. Some of this is due to the march of progress and the rise of the 'Farmers Mart', which allows animals to be traded all year round, but also I would suspect the rise of the regulators. The men who make the rules and regulations by which we live our lives and the men who probably don't see a herd of cows in the square as quaint or cute but more of a 'health and safety' issue. Maybe that is why the sheep have all but gone now and the poultry are just limited to the odd crate on the street corners, while the tractor trailers full of lively piglets, pink as fresh salmon are but a memory. Gone too are the red, painted carts pulled by the patient, faithful donkey and the farmer willing to walk maybe four miles into town with a reel of turf and a coat as black as the small Kerry cows that have trod many a weary mile to market. For even the cows now have to compete for parking spaces with the cars and seeing them side by side makes for an interesting analogy, for while a cow will throughout its life give you fresh milk in return for free, fresh grass and then at the end of its days give you beef. A car will get you from A-B, drink petrol at so-much a gallon, breakdown and eventually turn to rust to become an eyesore, abandoned in a country lane. Which I wonder is more precious?

Twenty years ago Main Street, Shelbourne Street and the Square would have been full of forlorn Heifers, harassed horses and prancing ponies trotting up and down, whilst a would-be buyer would decide on the condition, the energy and of course the price. In Kenmare on Fair Day there is no open auction, no farmer bidding against other farmers. More often that not it's done the traditional way. Just two men, who may or may not be friends finalising a deal over a drink in the favourite public bar. Whilst the cattle, oblivious to the traffic and the milling crowds, chew the cud and wait to be taken to pastures new. Then perhaps with the bonnet of a car serving as a 'bank clerk's counter', a cheque would be written and signed and handed over in place of hard cash. A sure sign that times were changing, but at least the car had its uses after all.

The 15th is certainly the Town's busiest day, trade in the shops restaurants, cafes and especially the bars is brisk to say the least. Any entrepreneur worth his salt using the double benefit of holiday and the crowds to chance his arm and make a few punts. The stalls that spring up around the town selling a wealth of useful, practical necessities for the farm. Kitchenware, saucepans, tools for the repairing of tractors, plenty of other farm implements and waterproof coats and Wellingtons that are always a good investment for the 'soft' days. Another popular stall is the second-hand clothes one in the square, though the 'open-air', as in the middle of the street, fitting room can afford visitors a few views of Kenmare that should never become postcards!

Fair Day is also a great one for families. Country cousins and Townies re-united for a few drinks and old friends to catch up on news that could be as much as a year old. It's also the time for special re-unions and that rare, once in a generation opportunity for life-long friends and relatives to come home for the holidays. It's not uncommon to meet people who have travelled from England and even America just to come back home to their birthplace or that of their parents. English nephews and American cousins witnessing first hand an event that has long been an important part of family folklore and will hopefully always remain a fixture on calendars and in hearts.

As the light fades and many drift back to the quiet of their farms already looking forward to the next feast of the assumption. In all twenty two bars in town the day is far from over and in the 'Kingdom' in Henry Street, reputed to be the best pub in town for music and dancing, the night is still young. Here in a very limited space, senior citizens defy their age, arthritis and gravity to give a spirited display of eight-some reels. A vivid reminder of the days when the 'crossroads' or the 'milk-churn stage' was the only place that Irish dancers and lone fiddlers could be free of the Church's disapproval.

For many, as the clock marches on to midnight. It will be time for the celebrating of a 'good' day or perhaps the bemoaning of another bad one, a drink to seal a deal or drown a sorrow. Though for most it will have been a great day, for some a 'fair' one, there will always be some old stager, leaning on his stick at the end of the bar, telling all who will listen how bad its been, how 'the devils have robbed him blind'. But he probably said that last August 15th and the one before that and the one before that...

For lovers of the game of Golf, Kenmare can offer one of the most beautiful courses in Ireland and for those that might consider the sport little more than; 'a good walk spoiled', the Golf club's location alongside 'the sound' to the west of the suspension bridge, and the magnificent views afforded every hole, easily makes it a worthwhile distraction to all that cursing of club and divot. It can also lead the unsuspecting visitor into one of Kenmare's best kept secrets, 'Reenagross', a natural park covering about 80 acres, that is tucked in between 'the sound', the Golf Club and the grounds of the Great Southern hotel. Access is gained either via the Golf club or a painted, green gate on the bridge road that though signposted, is all too easily missed by many flying past in their cars. But for those on foot or even bicycle who seek to satisfy their curiosity and investigate, it's a worthwhile detour.

'Reenagross' is a veritable haven from the hustle and bustle of the busy town. Literally just a stone's throw from the main Kenmare-Glengarriff road it has a rare natural beauty, a feeling of private seclusion and many a spot to sit or stand and contemplate views of sky, estuary and mountains that have scarcely altered in hundreds of years. It is also one of the best places to appreciate the wild birds that flock to 'the sound' to feed at low tide and maybe even glimpse an Otter or Heron competing for the title of best fisherman. But it's also a nice, quiet place to take a stroll, the council workmen having done much to create level pathways and even steps cut into the banks to allow access to the many vistas that wait around every twist and turn. One of the best being a view across the sound to another place of perfect peace, 'The Old Kenmare Graveyard.'

A couple of 'Irish miles' from Kenmare, the old Graveyard was the original site of 'Cean Mara'(head of the sea) a settlement that was established after the Beaker folk, about a thousand years ago. Set alongside both the Roughty and Sheen rivers, it was an excellent spot to catch fresh fish, and with plentiful reeds and timber close to hand one that allowed the construction of round huts that were more than capable of withstanding the harsh weather, but because of their natural construction have left precious little for today's archaeologists to investigate.

The Graveyard itself is still very much in use and boasts many a fine monument and memorial to the great and the good of Kenmare. The well tended gravestones like vast, granite books of family history, the names, dates and ages showing in graphic detail the hard lives endured by the people of Kenmare and the great respect that relatives still afford their ancestors. Sitting as close as it does to 'The Sound', the graveyard can be a bleak, exposed site on a raw, wet day in October with the wind and rain roaring in from the Atlantic. But on a soft, April morning with scarcely a breeze to rustle the tree's and just the distant call of the curlew to dent the solemn silence, it is a place to think, a place to remember and also a place to feel close to something that has no place in the crash and dash of modern life. Something that is as important as tomorrow, has as much significance and influence as today and something that should always be a reminder of where we come from and where we all ultimately end up. A graveyard like the step between today and yesterday, and the breath between yesterday and tomorrow.

Looking across 'The sound' from the stone wall of the Graveyard and looking more like an ancestral home than a place of residence for holidaymakers, stands the 'Great Southern Hotel 'or as it is now known, 'The Park Hotel'. Rising above the natural beauty of Reenagross, the Great Southern as most locals still refer to it, is an imposing grey-stone building that dominates the skyline from this side of the sound and yet is all but invisible from its entrance in Shelbourne Street. The relatively inconspicuous entrance flanked by tall tree's set, between The Police Station and Bookshop in such a way that were it not for the sign, you could pass straight by and never know it was there. It is one of those quirks of geography that could have proven to be something of a liability over the years, but then 'The Great Southern' was never a hotel that needed to announce itself; its reputation preceded it and ensured that it was and still is one of the finest places to stay in all Kerry.

There were five 'Great Southern' hotels in Ireland and all five were in Kerry. Apart from Kenmare, there were hotels at; Parknasilla, Waterville, Caragh Lake and Killarney. All of similar construction and quality, for some Kenmare's, designed by James Franklin Fuller of Glashnacree, was the most impressive. The south façade of the building that overlooked the impressive lawns and date palms offering some of the finest views in all Kerry. Almost every window afforded a stunning panoramic view of 'The Sound', Reenagross and beyond it Ballygriffin wood and the daunting rock slabs of Mucksna Mountain.

Inside the hotel it is no less impressive and for those that believe that an open fire gives off a sense of warmth, comfort and welcome, the lounge of the 'Great Southern would be a home from home, with a huge roaring fire welcoming guests all year round, summer and winter. Upstairs, the hotel boasts six master suites with huge four-poster beds and as the Ward & Locke Guide books used to say in 1899;'furnished with every modern comfort and convenience including electric light'. Something that was not to be taken for granted at a time when most of Kenmare was still lit by paraffin lamps and using outside toilets.

In 1899, Bed and Breakfast at the 'Southern' was six shillings and sixpence (32 new pence). Full board for the week was 70 shillings (£3.50) not an inconsequential sum in those days. In 1983, Bed and Breakfast costs £47 and the tariff for full board for seven days is £270. One just hopes that the visitors who can afford the luxury will not just look at the splendour around them that costs a small fortune and ignore the priceless views that cost nothing at all.

At the turn of the century 'The Great Southern' was a regular staging post for the four horse coaches favoured by well-to-do travellers in Ireland. These vehicles were very similar to the 'Bians' used by Charles Bianconi, an Italian print seller who settled in Clonmel in 1815 when a lot of brave Irishmen were dying on the battlefields of Waterloo in Europe. Bianconi soon had factories making the coaches and harnesses and is credited with the design of the Jaunting cars that are still used to this day in Killarney, as well as ten-seater cars where the passengers faced the hedgerows. Though the first coaches had wooden wheels it wasn't long before these were replaced with pneumatic tyres, hickory shafts and even sprung suspension. It was reputed that at the peak of his success Bianconi had up to 1,300 horses in service in Ireland, more than the British Army.

Even in relative comfort, the journey from Killarney to Kenmare took three and three quarter hours and with another three and a quarter until they got to their destination in Glengarriff, travellers who had paid fifteen shillings for a single fare, were only to happy to satisfy their appetites with a fine luncheon at the Southern, while horses were watered and coaches were subject to any running repairs that the fierce Kerry roads inflicted on springs and tyres.

The building of better roads in the 19th Century made way for the introduction of the Mail coach. During those days the Post Office was on Main Street opposite the 'Lansdowne Arms Hotel'. The mail was despatched from Kenmare at 3.30.a.m and at 9.30.p.m received the incoming mail from Killarney. For the Post Office workers the hours were very long but there was compensation in the knowledge that their job was much appreciated by all those that received letters from far-away relatives and perhaps a comforting word from a son or daughter in far off England or America.

Many roads in Kerry were the result of Famine Relief Projects, but were of huge value to people that had to Travel with any regularity. For example, the building of a road from Macroom to Glenflesk shortened the distance of a journey from Kenmare to Cork by 31 statute miles. A massive saving in terms of time and wear and tear on coaches, animals and humans. These new roads were often more direct and more in keeping with the demands of the modern traveller. The older roads built in the 18th Century had tended to go over hill and dale to many of the remotest farmsteads in valleys or on the mountain sides and were basic to say the least and often virtually impassable in really bad weather.

Of the new roads being built in the 19th Century, one of the finest mountain roads is the one from Lauragh to Ardgroom over the 'Healy Pass'. This pass which would be as at home in Switzerland as Ireland, was named after Tim Healy 1855-1931, 1st Governor General of the Irish Free State who had been born just over the Cork/Kerry border in Bantry.

The new road from Killarney to Kenmare, through 'Molls Gap' had been built in 1832 by Alexander Nimmo, the well known Scottish Engineer and Railway pioneer. The road which was something of an achievement in its day has since become a world famous route through some of the most beautiful scenery, not just in Ireland, but the world. And as a means of viewing Killarney's famous lakes has no rival. The views have given joy to countless thousands of people over the years and even the indomitable Queen Victoria had to linger awhile and give the title to a beauty spot that is known the world over, 'Ladies View'. It is a stunning spot looking down on the Gearhameen River which flows through the 'Upper Lake', the 'Long Range' and on to Muckross Lake. I'm sure that one of the greatest of all Queens would have been more than amused that a casual remark such as 'come Ladies and see the view' made to her travelling party all those years ago would still be a title for a view that is synonymous with Irish beauty and the majesty of nature. She must have been enchanted to see the rugged, wild landscape of Kerry after the subtle formality of Osbourne House on the Isle of Wight.

Alexander Nimmo was also responsible for the construction of the Glengarriff to Kenmare Road in 1823. Where he achieved his objective by managing to actually drill through the mountains themselves. The longest tunnel on the Cork/Kerry border is called 'Turners Rock' and is a staggering 250 yards long. A monumental achievement in any age it even has a ventilation shaft in the roof where daylight can be glimpsed that could be seen as the great man's anticipation of the problems connected with petrol fumes in years to come? Though there are two more tunnels on the Kerry side as you descend the mountain, they are but a few yards long and though no mean feat in terms of the ingenuity and man hours that went into constructing them, neither is a match for 'Turners Rock' and the skill of a great man who must have honed his tunnelling skill on the Killarney-Kenmare Road where were it not for the tunnel at Gortroe near the upper lake, there would have been no road at all.

For every new road saving time, effort and distance there is an old one falling into disrepair, but still used by the farmers who perhaps have no choice or the ramblers who find the old roads a more picturesque way of getting from A to B. One such case is the old Kenmare/Glengarriff road built in 1775. This had emanated from Kenmare, followed the Sheen River through Tullaha, Bonane and Garyletter then headed up and over the Flesk Mountains between Esk Mountain and Barraboy. Not far from this road on Canrooska is a 'Mass Rock', a reminder of penal times when the English throne held sway over the Protestant church and because of the politics of Religion decided that the Irish race should also come under their ruling. This made the celebration of a Catholic Mass illegal and with churches made utterly redundant, left the Priest with no other option than to head up into the mountains and using a large flat rock as an altar celebrate mass in the open air. Though people would travel many miles to attend there was a genuine risk. For if the authorities found out, anyone caught breaking this law could face prosecution, eviction or even transportation to the penal colonies of far off Australia!

Ten years later in 1785 a more direct route to Bantry was built. This left the older road in Gearha and went up and over the mountains via 'The Priest's Leap' at a height of 1,331 feet, before it dropped down to run parallel with the Cooleenlemane River all the way to the coast. Still a route that can be driven, it should be said that it is not a route for the faint-hearted and the magnificent views are often at the cost of frayed nerves and chewed fingernails. One farmer in a Bantry bar once remarked that though he was not averse to using the road as a short cut, he never did so in the fog, in the winter or without a pair of brown trousers!

The name of 'Priest's Leap' derives, so legend has it from an occasion when a Priest, en-route from Kerry to Bantry to visit a sick man, learnt on the summit that the man was no longer sick, but dying. Fearful that he might not arrive in time to give the poor man his last rites and ease his passing into the next world, he knelt down, prayed and then leapt the five miles to his destination in a single bound. Leaving prints of his knees and fingers on the rock upon which he landed close to the town. There are of course many other versions of how it got its name and being Ireland it is not uncommon for these claims to become more dramatic and fantastic as the night unfolds. The addition of some liquid lubrication not unknown to cause a few embellishments!

Though unique for different reasons any of the old roads could be a veritable nightmare for the more conventional four-wheel carriages, loose stones, pot-holes and axle-deep mud could make some roads virtually impassable at any time of the year and it was common practice for wise travellers to have four men on hand to physically push the carriage out of trouble, when and not if this occurred. One solution to this problem of getting bogged down was to revert to the two-wheel, Jaunting car that was the national vehicle of Ireland in the 1840's. Known to some as the 'Side-Car', because of the way passengers sat, two a side, facing outwards it was a multi-purpose vehicle and for those that could afford one and had a horse the ideal way to get to town for shopping, Mass and the all-important 'Fair Day'.

For most country folk who weren't even lucky enough to have even a donkey cart, the only way to get around was on foot or what some called 'Shank's Pony'. For many country people there really was no alternative and people would think nothing of walking six or seven miles into town for mass, or sending children five miles to school with just a couple of slices of home-made bread and butter for their lunch. Cars were an unheard of luxury well into the 1950's and bicycles were usually reserved for the 'mad' tourists sweating their way up to 'Windy Gap'.

Back in Kenmare and though not on quite the same scale as the 'Great Southern', another favoured watering hole for the Bianconi passenger coaches was 'The Lansdowne Arms'. Ideally situated right at the top of Main Street, there was plenty of space for coaches, travellers and those just curious to see who was passing through, or had come home for the holidays. Though more often than not it would be just holidaymakers or visitors from England or America. There were occasions when, as in 1858, the 'Lansdowne' afforded hospitality to Edward Prince of Wales, who later became King Edward VII, but not before travelling from Bantry to Killarney by Bianconi car and unwittingly giving the road the grand title of the 'Prince of Wales Route'.

But over the years Kenmare has been no stranger to the odd celebrity visit, the Lansdowne and Great Southern playing host to the likes of Thomas McCauley, the novelist, Sir Walter Scott, novelist and poet, William Wordsworth, poet, Arthur Young the agriculturalist, Charles Chaplin, the worlds greatest comic screen star, Sir Arthur Guinness, actor and film star and Bernard Lovell the scientist. It was also on one memorable occasion visited by Prince Rainer and Princess Grace of Monaco who, while staying at the Great Southern in Parknasilla, and seriously irritated by the constant attention of news reporters and photographers, decided to make the journey to Kenmare to buy shoes for the royal children and hopefully get some peace. But it wasn't to be, on arrival they soon found that someone had tipped off the press and they were so pestered by news reporters and photographers in the town that they had to cut short their visit and saw precious little of either Kenmare or the wilds of Kerry. A great shame for any visitor, but unfortunately some might say the price of fame.

At the other end of Main Street and just beyond the square is the Finnihy Bridge, originally built in 1715 it was widened in the seventies to accommodate the great increase in tourist traffic and now stands as a fine gateway to the town for visitors from Killarney or Sneem. Spanning the point at which the Finnihy River alters its course by ninety degrees to flow along the outskirts of town, past the stone circle and on towards the Kenmare River.

But just before the bridge and a quaint shop made entirely of corrugated iron that sells woollen products is a right turn. If you take it and go down past the Kenmare Creamery you come to a bend just before a row of pleasant cottages that are almost identical to those in Market street, and just past these is one of Kenmare's best kept secrets, a Holy shrine, known locally as 'Our Lady's Well'.

The entrance is through a wrought-iron gate which leads you onto a path that is sheltered on both sides by rocks and shrubs, then through a second gate and into the shrine itself. Here the shrine to Our Lady and the well is the centre of a circular path where it is the tradition for people of all ages to do' the rounds'.

Walking along the well-kept paths between the rocks and flowers while making their devotions to Mary, and especially on August the 15th, the feast of the Assumption. When doing 'the rounds' in the peace and calm of the holy well can seem like a veritable haven from the hustle and bustle of the Fair Day.

Our Lady's Well was originally the spring from which a group of Augustinian Monks got their fresh water supply some time in the 12th Century. Though with the nearby Finnihy being tidal, often the water was less than fresh. The

Monks lived in an Abbey that was sited on the other side of the Finnihy River about a mile away in an area known locally as 'The Shrubberies'. From here the Monks would have to commute via a semi-arched stone bridge (also known as a Rainbow Bridge) built entirely of local limestone and held together with only earth. That it still stands to this day and is still used a testament to its construction and the skill of the monks who made it with few tools and mostly just their bare hands. It is also the only reminder of the Augustinian Monks now as nothing remains of their Abbey and even the legacy that is the rainbow bridge has become confused with local people referring to the bridge as 'Cromwell's Bridge', when Oliver Cromwell neither set foot in Kenmare or the Kingdom that is Kerry.

Why this ancient masterpiece of bridge building should have become misnamed is a bit of a mystery. One theory is that someone over the years misinterpreted the Gaelic for carved wood - 'Cromcoll' as Cromwell or that the name did indeed stem from the time when Cromwell's 'Roundheads' built a fort just outside the town in 1853 and carried out their ritual burning of churches and homesteads? Once again, we cannot be sure though there is evidence of their dirty work having been committed near Kilcrohane near Waterville; in Kenmare neither fort nor Roundheads remain.

The 'rainbow' bridge also provided access in the 17th Century to Sir William Petty's iron smelting works at Gortamullen. Though a relatively crude process back then, the iron works was a prosperous business and provided work for the men of the town, though very much at the expense of the local woodland which then covered every acre from Kenmare to Lauragh. The fact that the furnaces had to be kept burning day and night giving you some idea of the timber that was needed and the impact this had on not just the countryside, but also anyone else that needed timber for homes, fences and furniture.

The ironstone, or to be more exact, the red-ore had to be imported from Wales, and then fed into the furnaces. When the right temperature was reached, the ore was tapped from the surface. Leaving the furnace like a molten river to run out into a series of channels laid out in the sand. The main run was called the 'sow' and the lesser tributaries that branched off it were the 'pigs', hence the name pig-iron. The waste that came from the tapping hole of the furnace was called 'slag'.

There are at least two of Petty's furnaces still in existence today and both are in good condition considering their age. The one most easily seen is on private farmland, just off the Killarney Road, about a mile from 'Saheleen Bridge', known locally as 'two mile bridge' for obvious reasons. The other lies about half a mile along the old 'bog road' which is just before the bridge and now has the dubious distinction of being the main access to Kenmare's refuse tip as well as the second home for hundreds of greedy gulls.

Before the Great Famine in 1845 there were only 65 miles of railway line in Ireland, twenty years later there were nearly 2000 miles and over the ensuing years the amount of main-line track continued to increase. So it was that in 1891 work began on the branch line from Headford to Kenmare. Built with financial aid from the British Government it was to be an extension of the 'Great Southern and Western Railway'. A single track, twenty miles in length, passing through the rugged, wild mountains and three small stations with quaint sounding names; 'Loo Bridge', 'Morley's Bridge'(something of a name-check for Ebenezer Scrooge's hard pressed partner) and 'Kilgarvan'.

When the line first opened there were three or even four trains a day and made jobs like the transportation of cattle on the 'Fair Day' significantly quicker and less wearing on the hoof. The journey time was about 60 minutes and was something of a boon for local trade, in that it was able to carry Butter to Cork butter Market and the home-spun wool of the Ashgrove and Gortamullen Mills to Cobh and onto England. It was also very beneficial to people too and on his second visit to Kerry in 1903, the Prince of Wales was one of many to use the branch line to Kenmare. It also opened up the possibility of travel to other parts of Ireland via the return journey to Headford Junction where passengers changed trains to carry on to Dublin in the east and Tralee in the west.

Though in the last eight years of its service there were just two trains a day, there was always great activity at Kenmare station at around 1.00.p.m when the main train of the day would come in bringing visitors, tourists and often relatives completing the last leg of their journey from far off England or America. Mind you when I say last leg, there was still the long haul by foot to the 'Great Southern' or 'Lansdowne Arms' while the luggage was despatched via Mr Bill Horgan and his very temperamental donkey and cart.

But not all journeys were to Kenmare. Over the years, Kenmare station must have been witness to a great many sad departures, the platforms stained with the tears of too many Irish parents who have been saying goodbye to their offspring for centuries. Reluctantly sending sons and daughters off to all parts of the world to make their fortunes and hopefully help those that they must leave behind. The Irish Diaspora as much a part of life then as it is today, the continued emigration and dispersion of its people a factor that sits hard with the relatives left behind, but one that guarantees the traveller a warm welcome around the world and a genuine 'Irish pub' in every city from Chicago to Bangkok.

But in later years as roads in Kerry and West Cork began to improve, so the railway began to suffer from stiff competition with Lorries who could get goods from farm to market or factory to dockyard and the motor car which could get traveller from boat to hotel without the temperamental donkey and cart, and as tourist use in particular began to decline in the late fifties. It was decided to close the line down and on December 31st 1959 Driver Paddy Dalton and John O'Rourke brought the last train into Kenmare where large crowds and even a Television crew were waiting to witness the end of an era. Though there were voices of dissent from those that relied upon the train, they were very much in the minority and the rails were lifted the following year.

Nowadays little remains of the Kenmare to Headford branch line, there is some evidence of where it had been in the valley beyond Kilgarvan, some landmarks that are definitely evocative of the railway's route, but precious little else. Back in Kenmare the site of the railways station is now occupied by a small factory of German ownership manufacturing plastic products in Railway road. The only real reminder is the Stationmasters house, a distinctive, bright, house of a pleasing design and character that stands out from the normal clay brick houses in that it is built of imported red bricks.

Looking back now with the benefit of hindsight, it's plain to see that the dear-departed branch line would have made for a great tourist attraction today. The lure of the Steam engine and the pre-war carriages almost definitely proving as much a draw as the restored line at Blennerville, near Tralee or the large numbers of similar projects in England and Wales. In such places, even a relatively small section of working branch line not only provides a piece of living history but can, quite literally, transport many an old schoolboy back to the joys of youth. Such projects usually attract huge support and with the tireless dedication of enthusiasts, are usually able to make a profit and turn a hobby into, not just a viable business and a reminder of better times, but a joy for children of all ages, and we are talking 6 to 60 here!

But with all the engines, carriages and even the rails themselves gone to the scrap-yards long ago, such a venture would be both a practical and economic impossibility and sadly the Kenmare to Headford branch line must be forever confined to the history books and the memories of those lucky enough to have made the journey.

Transportation and travel have always been a dominant force in the Irish nature and whether that journey be a walk to the next farm, a coach ride to the next town, a train ride to the next county or a boat ride to another country. The Irish have always been willing to venture outward, the Diaspora that has become a feature of so many lives seeming ingrained into the very spirit of men and women who, were it not for this wanderlust, might conceivably live out their entire lives in the shadow of the same mountain and never travel beyond the next river or glen.

Though some might claim that this is something inherited over centuries from the many wandering tribes that came to Ireland from Wales, Scotland and beyond. Brave souls who were not afraid to brave rough seas in small boats and then still had the tenacity to carve out a life in a landscape that does not make gaining a foothold easy. Others would say that it was circumstance that made the Irish a nation of rovers, and the Diaspora we talk of is not instinctive but borne of necessity and the pressures placed on men and women by Invaders, enemies and natural disasters.

For such a relatively small country stuck out on the furthest most edge of Western Europe, Ireland has been a party to some of the most dramatic fluctuations in population, very few of them the result of natural phenomenon or even Famine.

For if you scratch the surface of the emerald Isle even a little, you will find war and conflict in abundance. The Irish history books crammed to bursting with tales of battles, bloodshed and blight. But, even though much misery was wrought by the Irish upon the Irish, in the 17th Century in particular the population was practically decimated by events taking place beyond its own shores.

For example in September 1610, 600 Irishmen were despatched to serve the Swedish crown in foreign wars. Between 1641-1642, over 40,000 men, women and boys, and even 6000 priests were deported to Spain, France and Flanders to serve in and service various armies, and another 10,000 were transported to Barbados as slaves.

The following year 250 women aged between 12-45 years and 300 men of similar age were transported to the West Indies. In 1655, 1000 Irish girls were shipped into slavery in Jamaica. Sir William Petty, Oliver Cromwell's Surveyor General, reckoned that between 1641 and 1652 half of Ireland's population of 1,460,000 had been exiled or exterminated. It was reckoned that if all the tears that had been shed over so many lost souls throughout the centuries were gathered in one place at one time, there would be a lake to rival Muckross itself.

In later years Famine did much to decimate the population of Ireland and a national census in 1851 revealed that the population had fallen by more than a quarter, the missing people numbering 2,400,000. Though many of these were emigrants that had fled to foreign lands to escape poverty and fever. It was believed that the Famine had cost 1,100,000 lives and in some rural area's whole villages were wiped out. After 1851 emigration continued to account for a declining population with another 5,000,000 men, women and children leaving Ireland in the next sixty years. In 1911 the population of Ireland was half of what it had been in 1845.

CHAPTER SIX.
The Old Road- The Fever Hospital - Booley Villages

In all, eight roads converge on Kenmare and as you might expect in the tourist season this can create the sort of traffic jams to give any Gardai a king-size headache and have a Traffic warden rubbing his hands with glee. But, though there are times when the town does indeed resemble a very large, triangular car park and the 500 yard journey from the square to the Bell Heights can take anything up to half an hour, everybody eventually gets by. Anyone arriving in town on an August afternoon would do well to heed the old moral of 'patience being a virtue' and consider the slow crawl through Kenmare as a rare opportunity to see the sights and make note of a few fine hostelries and pubs. There is no detour, no by-pass and no point getting all worked up. The town of Kenmare doesn't even have a traffic light to curse, so just go with the flow enjoy your crawl down Henry Street or up Main Street, it's not like you have a choice.

Many towns and villages in Kerry share the same traffic problems. Even on the well-travelled Ring of Kerry, towns such as Sneem and Waterville can seem like badly designed bottlenecks or even actual 'tourist traps' at times. But you have to remember that this isn't some Celtic plot to dissuade visitors from travelling along Irish roads or some scheme to slow everybody down to a super-safe five miles per hour. It is in fact geography and the simple fact that many towns are where they've been for centuries and the road is where it is, because there is nowhere else for it to go. Mountains, rivers, valleys and the sea call the shots.

The scenery determines where the roads go in Ireland and the scenery also determines how fast you go through it. The dearth of traffic lights and roundabouts on the Ring of Kerry is no accident. For when the traffic is compelled to slow down in the built up area's, you don't actually need them.

But for those who perhaps want to get away from it all, go one better and escape the confines of both car and contra-flow, one worthwhile alternative is the old road from Kenmare to Killarney.

It is a road full of history and both kinds of memories and could well be one of the oldest roads in Kerry. Mind you it's not what you could call easy-going, as time, the weather and years and years of feet and cart-wheels have taken their toll. Nowadays the latter half from Gulway's ford to Muckross Village is hardly traceable and most of the other half is barely fit for walking. But it is worth the wear and tear on legs and leather, there simply is no other way to see many of the views on offer and whether you're a rambler, naturalist, historian or maybe just a seeker after peace and quiet in a hectic, noisy world, the old road has something very special to offer. If you still feel up to the challenge that is?

Starting in the Square, head north on Railway Road out past the Holy Cross church, the turning to Scarteen Park and towards what locals call the 'Hospital road', it's a long straight, steady climb and about a mile out of town you reach the Dromneavane road. On your left stands what appears to be a row of two storey houses. Built of limestone and covered in crawling Ivy they are indeed quite attractive these days. But would not have seemed so in the past when this was in fact, the old Kenmare Fever Hospital and a building many poor folk would only ever see once as they were carried in.

It had opened in the spring of 1847 at a time of great

suffering for the people of Kenmare and in charge was a man who needed to be true to his vocation, one Doctor Thomas Taylor. At this time the Famine was at its height and as you might imagine the hospital was soon full of unfortunate souls suffering the agonies of dysentery, diarrhoea, anasarca and dropsical infection of the limbs. But with so many patients to contend with, the hospital soon ran out of beds and doctors and nurses had no choice but to lay fever patients out on straw alongside the dead and the dying. The overcrowding was compounded by the fact that the nearby 'Union Workhouse', that stood on the site of the present hospital and had only been open for two years, was also crammed full to bursting. It was a desperate situation that would not have been made any easier had there been a dozen more hospitals within the district. The Famine was just too much to cope with in any circumstances and in the end the devoted doctors and nurses were simply overwhelmed and unable to even treat, never mind cure most of the victims and all they could do was to try and help to ease the passing, which for too many poor souls was already a foregone conclusion.

Though over the next few years some medical progress was made in the treatment of Famine victims and with the help of the Famine Relief Fund, fewer died of starvation, it was the fever that still claimed most lives and without impunity. Charles Peter Thomas curate of St.Patricks one of many to die of the fever in June 1847 aged 45 years.

In those terrible years the fever hospital, like the union work house was always crowded to suffocation and it is reckoned that at least 5000 men, women and children died of the famine between 1845 and 1849 in Kenmare alone. One notable victim being the good Doctor, Thomas Taylor who died on the 4th of February 1848, barely a year after taking charge. His death showing graphically the risks that Doctors, nurses and their auxiliaries took in their vocational desire to help others. They were not the only ones to help. Both local priests were regular visitors to the Hospital and workhouse, offering spiritual as well as practical help when it was needed and the last rites when it was too late. Their presence a real comfort to the miserable wretches who could live with the threat of death but not die without their God. But their vocation was not without its risks and every time the priests entered hospital, workhouse or homes they were at the mercy of any number of contagious diseases, many fatal as the death of the curate of St.Patricks clearly showed.

But for Father John O'Sullivan, the risks came with the job and he was never going to let selfish fears prevent him from doing God's work. Almost on a daily basis he would witness scenes of human suffering that were of the most abject misery and degradation. At the height of the famine it wasn't uncommon to find victims lying dead in the ditches where they fell. A rank, soaking hollow in the barren earth becoming their last resting place on this earth.

For many it was their homes that became their tomb, the humble cabin with neither window nor chimney and just a mud floor that flooded when it rained, a cruel unforgiving place to live out your last days, too weak to light a fire, never mind cook the Indian corn that was no substitute for the precious potatoes. It was not uncommon for the good Father to visit many of these 'Byres' and find whole families dead in their beds.

The Famine must have put a great strain on the faith of many who saw no respite from the suffering, but Father O'Sullivan was not one of them. Though a man of God whose job it was to offer spiritual comfort for the sick and the dying, he never forgot the practical needs of the living, even to the extent of personally importing corn from England. In a time of great need, when whole towns were paralysed with hunger and despair he did all that he could and more and the people of Kenmare owe both the priest and the man a great debt. That like the suffering of the Irish people should never be forgotten.

Throughout the rest of Ireland, the same famine claimed the lives of over 200,000 people. For many there had been no medical care, no coffin and no priest to read the last rites. Their final resting place, in most instances just a mass grave in unconsecrated ground with no marker or stone. To this day no-one actually knows how many Famine graves exist and it was only in 1982 that a mass grave was discovered in Kenmare's burial ground and marked by those that remember and care with a white memorial.

They say that this stretch of the 'old road' where many victims of the famine trod their last steps to Hospital and Workhouse is haunted by the ghosts of their poor, tormented souls. And while yes on certain days you can be overcome with a palpable feeling of melancholy as you pass the road to Dromneavane, there are no spectral figures to be seen, nor banshee cries to be heard. Just a solemn, sobering memory of all those that died in those terrible years and of the legacy of Famine that haunts Ireland and its people and always will.

It's a fairly fierce climb once you get above Dromneavane; the road is almost as straight as a Roman road and finally peaks at some 638 feet above sea level. But once you get there you know it's been worth it as you stare out at what could be one of the best panoramic views in all Kerry.

Looking east are the distant Mountains between the Slaheny and Sheen rivers and the Roughty valley with Kenmare already in the near distance. Towards the west, Boughil rises from the valley floor to be dwarfed by the magnificent ridges of Magillycuddy's Reeks, or 'Cruacha Vic giolla muchooda' in Irish, that dominate the skyline like a rugged trademark for the wilds of Kerry.

Up ahead to the north-east stands Mangerton, a beautiful 'whale-backed' mountain that with its gently moulded slopes looks to have escaped the rugged forces of the ice age. But not so Peakeen and its companion Knockanaguish that look as though they have been physically expelled from the earth to stand silent sentinel on the old road that passes directly between them. Here just a mile and three quarters from the town, as the sun catches the shadows of the clouds it feels like another world, the peace and quiet broken only by the shrill calls of the linnets as you stare out on the rugged patchwork quilt that seems to adorn both mountains, before folding gently back into the valley.

As you walk on through grass covered hills full of nonchalantly munching cows, Inchimore on the right and Lissyclearig on the left it's easy to understand what it is that has drawn writers, artists, photographers and lovers of nature to this precious corner of the world. For even now, just a few minutes later as you glance up towards Peakeen the reflections of the sunlight and the delicate shading of the clouds have changed the stone of the mountain from a grainy grey to a metallic purple.

It's a product of the ever changing Irish light that has both inspired and confounded artists for centuries, the same mountain viewed at different times of the day appearing to change from a cold grey to a warm, almost chocolaty brown.

Leaving the old road for just a minute, it is well worth the half mile diversion to the top of Lissyclearig to take in a magnificent panoramic view of the Kenmare River stretching all the way from Our Lady's Bridge to the Atlantic itself. On any day the view is breathtaking and on a bright clear one affords photographers and artists alike something unique to record for posterity. The early morning, before the haze of the day has had a chance to build up, is the best time. Then it is possible to see the Bull lighthouse standing 300 feet above sea level and stood three miles from the mainland. Nearby you can also see the Dursey head and a land mass called the Cow which is two miles from the Bull. Though there is another land mass called the calf, it must have strayed from its parents as you cannot see it from Lissyclearig.

This spot is also, it should be said, one of the finest spots in all Kerry to witness a sunset where the fading light of the dying day is at its most sublime. The clean, un-polluted Kerry air adding, so I'm told, a few more shades to the normal compliment of colours.

Returning to the old road, you now start to descend towards the Gowlane crossroads. Some locals claim that somewhere in this area is a stone marking the grave of an English soldier who was killed in the troubles of 1922, but with no precise location given and the ground littered with many stones it is unlikely that anyone will ever find it, if it does indeed exist. At the crossroads stands the now derelict Gowlane National School, the pupils long since having been transferred to the school in Kenmare. From here it is possible to take a different route back to Kenmare around the base of Lissyclearig or take the right fork, and providing the hiker has plenty of stamina, head on up to the 'Horses Glen'.

Looking up at Mangerton from the old road you'd be forgiven for thinking that the Horses Glen even existed, the mountain so smooth and gentle that the very idea of something rough and rugged clawed from its surface was one of those old tales you'd get from farmers who knew you were never going to go there. But, if you can make the trek up past Knockbrack and on to the summit of Mangerton Mountain itself you are in for a natural treat.

The Horses glen, so named because it was once a haven for wild horses that roamed the Kerry hills is about a 1000 feet below the summit and sat between Lough's Managh and Garagarry. It was created about a 150,000 years ago during the ice age, the glacial action of the rock resulting in a basin that looks like its been scooped out by some giant hand. The Redstone rock rising in sheer ribs from the Lough that nestles in the very bottom, the hillsides covered in Oak, Birch, Mountain Ash, Holly and an abundance of Arbutus.

To fully appreciate the majesty of the moraines and corries and see for yourself how the land was formed all those years ago, you have to go up to the top of Mangerton Mountain an extinct volcano which at 2756 feet above sea level gives you a clear view of the Glen, Lough's Managh and Garagarry, Lough Erhogh and the Owengarriff River which links all three. It is a spectacular view in anybody's language and a landscape that is not just the product of ancient history. For in 1903 there came a deluge so fierce that it washed away much of the peat bogs that used to adorn the summit and turned the three Lough's and the Owengarrif river a deep brown for over a fortnight. Though nature has long since covered up much of the evidence of the terrible deluge, you can in places still see table-top mounds of turf that hint at the force of the water that roared down the mountain carrying all before it.

A dangerous enough job in normal circumstances, working a bog on any mountain was hard work, working the bog at the top of Mangerton must have been very, very, hard labour indeed. First there was the arduous trek to get to the top, then the cutting of the turf in an area that was about as exposed to the elements as you were likely to get, the drying and then in the Autumn. The precipitous task of getting it down to the lowlands by a Donkey with two baskets slung on either side of his back. It was a slow and tedious job and when Donkey's sometimes did what Donkey's can do and lived up to their sometime stubborn reputation, it was left to women to carry the turf down in baskets upon their backs. A job that should not be underestimated when you think how hard it is to walk down any mountain, never mind do so with a couple of hundredweight of turf just itching to trip you up.

Another feature of the Mountain landscape is the coarse grass, the country folk call 'Fenane'. If cut at the end of June, beginning of July it can be saved just like hay and makes excellent winter fodder for cattle but not horses who will not touch it under any circumstances. If however the Fenane is left until August, the grass grows white, hard and firm, then loses all its sap and become loose at the roots. It is then of no use as the cattle will not eat it.

The Fenane of Mangerton is known by the country people as 'The Hungry Grass' and perhaps hints at the desperation of starving people in centuries past trying to eat what even their livestock would not. It is certainly for locals a reminder of the terrible hungry times and to stave off the hunger in future years. Superstitious locals' crossing over Mangerton through the 'hungry grass' would always take off their coats and turn them inside out.

A quarter of a mile from Mangerton's summit is the main source of Kenmare and Killarney's water supply, the 'Devil's Punch Bowl'. Another huge basin scooped out of the rock by glacial action, this crater it is reputed to be 700 feet deep and the water itself is an eerie, inky black colour. It is also a fine spot to get a great view of Muckross Lake, the Long Range and the studded isles of Lough Leane, and one where you're unlikely to be troubled by passing coach parties, so every drop of sweat expended on the way up will certainly be paid back in full with majestic beauty that many visitors will never see. It is also from the Devil's punchbowl that you get a fine view of Torc Mountain and perhaps your first glimpse of Killarney and the distant spire of St.Mary's Cathedral.

Apart from an abundance of pure, fresh, Irish water another interesting by-product of the Punchbowl is 'Whetstone', a natural mineral that used to be used for sharpening the old-fashioned and sinister-sounding, 'Cut-throat' razors.

About twenty years ago, a German structural engineer had plans to build a chair lift up to the Devil's Punchbowl, of the same design as those used in Alpine ski resorts; it was to run from the Killarney road at the base of Torc Mountain, all the way up to the Punchbowl. Though the idea never bore fruit and might well have been a legitimate way for many to experience the views from up on Mangerton. It is hard to imagine what the area would be like now, had it been turned into a tourist trap it certainly would not be the remote and rugged haven it still is twenty years later. And would the views be as special or as appreciated without the physical effort of getting up there to see them, I think not.

It is probably fair to say that the only true way to fully appreciate the magnificent mountain views of Kerry is with an ache in your calves and the sweat of effort upon your brow. Such powerful vista's deserve something in return and should be the reward for a two hour trek through bog and wet grass and not some distant photo-opportunity glimpsed through a coach window at thirty miles an hour. The Iveragh, Beara and Dingle peninsula's are at the very heart of a region that was born only through the most violent of the east and west foldings of the earth's crust. A folding that was the result of immense north and south pressure at the close of the 'Carboniferous' period, and while the overlaying beds of limestone were washed away in solution by the sea and now remain for the most part only in the valleys. The harder slates and rocks of the older, underlying Devonian strata endures to form the wild mountain ridges that are the crowning glory of the Kingdom of Kerry.

It is while in places such as this that the traveller is liable to not only forget the noise and aggravation of 'civilisation' but the passing of time itself, and not just the few hours since breakfast or the few until dinner. Hundreds of feet above the towns and the roads you are in a landscape that is thousands and thousands of years old and might look exactly the same today as it did a hundred years ago. This high up man has yet to make even a dent in the eco-structure, never mind make his mark on the land and as such is as insignificant as the insects buzzing around the Fenane. In a world where Mankind has in many places already destroyed much natural habit and irrevocably scarred views and vista's that can never be replaced or reclaimed. It is of great comfort to stand in a spot upon a mountain side, staring at a view that man will never be able to spoil, the vast rugged wilderness that is much of the west coast of Ireland. Perhaps a reminder of greater powers at work, a timescale in which three score years and ten are but a heartbeat and a subtle humbling of Mans desire to change the world around him because Man thinks he knows better. In Ireland and most especially in Kerry it is reassuring to know that Man comes way down a list that begins with the powers of Nature, weather, the seasons and even God himself. And if that sounds a little pompous, then might I suggest that you've never stood in the depths of the 'Black Valley' as a summer storms rears up over the heights of the Macgillycuddy's Reeks, turning the sky the colour of night as white lightning stabs from the clouds and thunder roars through the peaks like the mountains themselves were moving. For if you had and then seen a beautiful rainbow arching above the valley floor, well you would be in no doubt whatsoever as to who's the boss, no doubt at all.

In the old days, most mountain roads had only one purpose and that was to provide access to the remote, isolated farms in far off valleys and glens. These were simple, rough tracks that went over hills instead of around them, through streams instead of over them and were in the most part just a one way route from here to there and back again. An old, sheltered farm house standing at the end of what is to all intents and purposes just a dead end. Kerry is full of them and to the un-initiated hiker they can be a bit of a nightmare in terms of wasted walks and re-traced footsteps. Especially when at the end of your wasted walk you are unable to see the Farmhouse that could be nestling in a natural hide out of trees and bushes just a few yards away.

Though any Farmer worth his salt could tell you where to look, how to find a site that is sheltered from the east winds but in such a position as to take full advantage of the natural light. Often it is only the barking of a friendly Collie dog that gives them away, the trees and bushes that give shelter just as surely camouflaging window and chimney pot. But even these homesteads, already rare as hen's teeth, are becoming even rarer. For as the old methods of farming die out and sons and nephews are reluctant to leave the towns, the old farms are left to the mercy of the elements and are fast falling into disrepair. Wasted homes at the end of a wasted walk.

Back at the Gowlane crossroads, the right hand fork is one such dead-end and that's after a mile walk to an isolated farm by the Cummeenboy Stream. Though on a fine summer's day it would be cruel to call this a 'wasted walk' as the views, the scenery and the peace is well worth every step. It does give the visitor some idea of what it must have been like for the Farmer, his wife and their children who could not' just nip to the shops', or 'pop around the corner', but instead had to endure an eight mile walk into town and eight miles back, a veritable trek that even with practice would take the better part of a day, and that was in good weather. On a 'soft' November day with the rain stinging your face and soaking your clothes it would have been a real endurance test and a testament to the resilience of country folk who might endure such hardship on a daily basis.

Beyond the farmhouse, the dead-end road carries

on for three miles and offers splendid views of the Irish Forestry's plantings on the slopes of Coombane and Knockbrac mountains. Though a stiff 2,139 foot climb, from the summit of Knockbrac there are excellent views of Mangerton and the fifteen lakes that lay scattered around the peak of Dromeralough. Somewhere between the beautifully named Lough Naheisknagirramy and its neighbour Lough Keamnabricka is 'The Bishop's Chair' a piece of natural stone that resembles a mighty throne and another of the 'Mass Rocks' that had been the last bastions of Catholic faith in Elizabethan times.

These are wild places and the keen hiker is unlikely to set eyes on another human being for hours at a time, though to be honest you will never be entirely alone as there are always the curious mountain sheep to offer a bit of distant company. Many, many years ago, about 14,000 to be precise, this would have been the domain of the 'Irish Red Deer', an impressive beast that stood over six feet tall at the shoulder. But, more incredibly had antlers that could be 9 feet wide. When you think that a Canadian Moose's antlers are at best only 6 feet across, it gives you some idea of the scale of this magnificent creature. But also hinted at its biggest problem and probably one that helped to contribute to its downfall. For with a full set of antlers, the male deer often had problems negotiating trees, other obstacles and even just keeping its balance. Often if it fell down or became entangled it would be unable to regain its feet or help itself and subject to the cruel rules of nature Hunter became hunted and it often died where it had fallen. Though deer still roam the mountains of Kerry and herds of wild deer are a common sight on the slopes around Torc, they aren't quite on the same scale as their huge ancestor and probably with good reason. Their no less impressive, but significantly smaller antlers showing in living form the benefits of evolution.

Travelling straight ahead at the Gowlane crossroads, the old road changes to a more rugged, uneven surface that is more footpath than road and only fit for walking now. About a mile on you are about a thousand feet above sea level and in a prime position to climb one of the old road's 'sentinels', Peakeen, one of the most distinctive mountains this side of the Reeks. A steady but determined climb will get you to the cairn at the top, where at 1825 feet you are rewarded with magnificent views of 'The Church of the Sloe' otherwise known as Killarney to the north east beyond Mangerton, 'The little nest' or Kenmare to the south, the distant Kenmare bay joining company with the Atlantic and not forgetting the magnificent profile of the Reeks that dominates every view to the north west.

From the top of Peakeen nearly half of the old road can be clearly seen from Kenmare, through Dromneavane, Gowlane, Incheens and on to Gulway Bridge. It's only when you get to the stretch running alongside Cromaglan Mountain that it finally disappears from view as by then much of its surface has been obliterated by nature's reclamation of the land and is now all but gone. The faint trail that is left dictated by the wonderfully titled Esknamucky Glen and covered in grass.

It is also possible from this height to see the main Kenmare-Killarney road and the ceaseless throng of tourist traffic climbing up to Moll's Gap. While for many, this is the only civilised way to see the scenery. In a nice car, travelling in comfort and at a speed that makes walking seem almost stationary in comparison. Only pausing for a few minutes at the pre-requisite 'beauty spots' for the pre-requisite family photo then pressing on to Killarney for lunch. But in all truth it is no way to see the country at all. By sticking slavishly to the tarmac roads you miss much more than you ever see and of course though you can travel forty, fifty miles in a day, your only exercise is the few steps you make to take the same photo as everyone else or the ten yards to the gift shop to buy a postcard, for those who find even taking a photograph too taxing.

But if the cars and their passengers miss so much, the coaches who have come to 'do the ring' often see even less. Chained to an itinerary that dictates every stop and break in the journey. These travellers often get no more than a glimpse of Kerry's wild terrain and sat in a luxury coach on a hot, summers day with a fine Irish Breakfast and a liquid lunch in their belly's are often by late afternoon, far too busy dozing in their comfortable seats to even glimpse the spectacle of the sun catching the surface of a glass Lough and turning purple and green Mountains to a gentle, liquid blue.

One of the most distinctive features of Peakeen and a very familiar, man-made element of this rugged, rural landscape are the dry stone walls that divide up the mountain side, define farm boundaries and turn the mountain itself into a living patchwork of fields. Very similar in style, appearance and construction to those of Yorkshire and Northumberland in England, the dry stone wall is a classic example of man's ability to utilise an abundant, natural resource and with the help of a bit of time and a lot of skill, create something that is both a functional boundary and a thing of aesthetic beauty. Because they are made of natural, local stone and use no cement they sit better in the landscape and are soon colonised by plants, insects and animals. It's also worth noting that they are easier to repair and last considerably longer than their clay counterparts.

The old road has now reached its highest point of 1063 feet above sea level and starts to drop down into another haven of perfect peace beside the Villains River. To the left is 'Windy Gap', not to be confused with 'Molls gap' and beyond it the Glasloughs which has become a popular grazing ground for the Red deer which normally roam the heavily wooded areas around Torc Mountain. This would have been the ideal habitat for their ancestors, with its lush grasslands, abundance of fresh water and relative isolation from man and his weapons.

As the road continues to descend it is possible to glimpse the remains of an old settlement hidden amongst the undergrowth. Built almost entirely of stone and at least 200 years old, the small cabins crumbling walls still bare testament to the skill of the men that built them and even though the timber roofs have long since rotted away, it is possible to still get an idea of the hard lives these people must have endured. A little further on and set maybe 200 yards back from the road, a large clump of Rhododendron bushes hide the ruins of a larger building that might have been a well-to-do homestead. This Byre, like the other buildings is made of the same stone and utilises the same dry-stone technique of construction but has suffered more at the hands of the weather and the years. Even so its name is still remembered as the dwelling of the 'Woman of the Goats', and this in turn gives more than a hint of the type of farm it would have been.

As recently as thirty years ago, Goats were a familiar sight in the South Kerry countryside and at one time much of the western slopes of Mangerton were home to a large number of wild, black and white goats and only last year in 1982 it was still possible to see small family groups of wild goats among the steep crags around Boughil Mountain, close to the high road to Sneem, which was once dubbed the loneliest road in all Kerry.

As the old road continues to descend, you now find yourself in a fertile valley, the road criss-crossed with various streams that in summer represent no great hazard, but can in winter time be at least a foot deep in places and probably qualify as Fords. At one time of day, this road would have been a fairly busy thoroughfare for local people getting to and from their daily toil, but is now largely deserted as there is only one inhabited farmhouse in the whole valley. It is a quiet place of serene natural beauty and the last place you would think would have a bit of a past, a bit of a reputation. But once upon a time this valley was notorious as the place where the Poteen was made.

For those that do not know, Poteen is the Irish equivalent of moonshine or hooch. A form of homemade whiskey that is made from barley and is reputed to be 100% proof, strong enough to get a man blind-drunk in no time at all and very, very illegal. It was always popular in rural areas where 'proper whiskey' was too expensive for most and could be made with the most basic of 'stills' for a pittance. Though very strong, the drinking of Poteen also came with a number of health risks, apart from the obvious one of being drunk in an area where a step off the beaten track could result in a fall into Lough or crevasse. The strength of the drink could also in extreme cases actually cause permanent blindness. It also came with all the attendant social ills of strong drink and especially the impact drinking could have on families in terms of poverty and violence, or even imprisonment if you were caught by the Revenue men or the Gards.

Though the legal manufacturers and the inventors of Whiskey were keen to put the illegal stills out of business on trumped up social and moral grounds, it was really just so that people could drink themselves to death with their own brand rather than someone else's. If however you were looking for someone whose objection to Poteen was on moral grounds and who's only vested interest was in your soul, then you had to go back to 1938 and Father Mathew, a superior in the 'Capuchin order', who founded the 'First Irish Total Abstinence Association'. In a country known to partake of a drop from time to time, it was a seemingly ill-fated cause but because of the influence of the church had significant successes. The 'Apostle of Temperance' honoured with a statue in Cork City, close to St.Patricks Bridge and also a beautiful, Gothic church on the quay called 'The Father Mathew Memorial Church'.

At the end of the 'Villains River' valley near to where the old road crosses the Gulway river is the 'Shaking rock'. Close to this is a good stretch of made-up road which offers a slight detour down towards the main Kenmare - Killarney road and 'Gulway Bridge' which stands next to an abandoned catholic chapel. Only a mile or so below the famous 'Ladies View', the bridge is an excellent spot to get a photograph of the river as it tumbles down over the rocks towards the Upper Lake, but a spot where you are unlikely to be on your own as it is now a featured stop on the tourist trail and one of the last, safe parking places for cars until you reach Torc Waterfall. At this point, should you need to know it, you are 10 miles from Kenmare via the new road but only 6 miles via the old road.

Getting back on track, the old road now skirts the edges of Cromaglan Mountain and leads you into the Esknamucky Glen which follows the course of the Crinnagh River.

At the turn of the century, this area would have abounded with Japanese red deer and though their numbers had all but declined by the mid 20th Century, recent efforts to import a slightly more domesticated strain have been successful and numbers are on the increase. These 'Sika' deer free to roam the glen, Torc Mountain, 'The Bourne Vincent Memorial Park' and the Muckross Demesne. They are also a common sight for motorists and are often seen grazing on the very verges of the main Killarney road.

The 'Muckross Estate' was once owned by the Herbert family before it was passed on to Lord Ardilan and then onto Mr.Arthur Vincent an American senator who together with his parents in law, Mr and Mrs William Bowers-Bourne, created the 'Bourne Vincent Memorial Park' which covers over 10,000 acres and represents virtually all the land around the Muckross Estate. A substantial land package and an area of outstanding natural beauty it was given to the Irish Government and under their management has become a major tourist attraction visited by hundreds of thousands of tourists every year.

Muckross House, which was designed by the Scottish architect William Burn and built in 1843, was also a popular attraction in the 19th Century when the Herbert family played host to Queen Victoria, Prince Albert and four of their children in August 1861. Sadly this must have been one of the last Royal Family holidays as Prince Albert passed away only four months later. But it was a happy one, and most definitely a visit that has left an indelible mark on the area. Though the Royal Family also stayed at Kenmare House in Killarney at the behest of Lord Castleross. It was the Herbert Family that pulled out all the stops and had a cottage built for Queen Victoria on the Killarney road near Derrycunnihy. Though she only stayed in Killarney for a short time, the cottage has since been known as 'The Queen's Cottage', a section of the old road is still called the 'Queen's Drive' and of course it was Queen Victoria herself who in asking her ladies in waiting, 'to come see the view'. Established 'Ladies View' as one of the most prestigious views in all Ireland.

Unfortunately it was rumoured that the cost of playing host to Royalty all but ruined the Herbert Family financially and led to them selling the estate to Lord Ardilan. The only memory of the family now being a large Celtic cross that is dedicated to Henry Arthur Herbert 1815-1865 and stands close to the road to Lough Guitane. The other residence the Queen stayed at, Kenmare House in the shadow of St.Mary's Cathedral, was burnt down in the troubles between 1921-1922.

The section of the old road near Cores hill is an area like many in Kerry that is steeped in memories; unfortunately in this instance the memories are bad. For the people who once lived there had been the victims of 'The Clearances', a phrase that for the Irish people conjures up images as painful and cruel as anything the Famine could offer and just as catastrophic.

The area of land between here and the Muckross Estate was then owned by the Herbert Family and when the new road to Killarney was opened in 1823, it was decided that the old road should be closed to make way for a deer park. Thus enabling the visiting gentry to hunt without the distraction or interruption of the tenant farmers who happened to live there.

So to make a more suitable environment for the hunt, the valley was cleared. Bridges were demolished, crops spoiled and the people themselves evicted from their stone cabins without mercy, never mind provision for where they might go or how they might survive. The inhumanity of the English landlords was however not uncommon, the humble tenant farmers had always suffered at the hands of their rich masters. Even when Famines raged in Ireland and people starved in the streets, it was not a rare thing to be evicted from your home for non-payment of rent. The sick and the dying 'put out' because they had neither the money to pay, nor the strength to work. The English Landlords not content with exporting every last grain of corn from a starving country, but seeming intent on squeezing every last drop of blood from the poor, impoverished souls that often had to subsist in Hedgerows, until the elements, the famine or the fever claimed their miserable souls.

The Clearances were no different and as the splitting of cabin doors echoed through the Glen, and the battering ram did its vile work we can only wonder as to the consciences of the men who gave the orders. Men whose cruel response, when asked where tenants with neither money nor land to work might go to seek shelter, was to utter 'that there was always the workhouse'.

The only evidence left of the Clearances now are the piles of stones that had once been homes, a cruel reminder of man's inhumanity to man. For after splitting the cabin doors it was common practice to demolish or fire the roof and with just the walls still standing, leave nothing that could be a legitimate shelter for man or beast. In some parts of Ireland, evicted tenants were allowed to take their roof timbers with them, something that in a land that had often been stripped of all trees was a rare act of charity and meant that tenants could hang onto items that were sometimes deemed so precious as to be handed down from fathers to sons as legacies.

Further along the old road, still close to Cores Hill and where two streams meet to form the Crinnach River is a place called 'The Inch of the Town of Cows', which is reputed to the site of a 'Booley' village where drovers would live during the summer months close to their herds that grazed the surrounding hills from May to October. The word Booley coming from the Irish word buaile that means the movement of cattle to summer pasture.

Beginning on May Day, the drovers would live in the make-shift village for six months until All Hallows Eve or Halloween as we now know it. The men went up first to build the huts; there were usually six in a cluster in a 'Booley' village. They were built of sods of turf or rocks on a foundation of earth and stones. They were usually just one room measuring 15 feet by 9 and could be oval in shape or rectangular with rounded corners. The roof was constructed of unseasoned, green timber which was fine for what amounted to a temporary structure, the timbers covered with long strips of turf and thatched with leather secured by hand-made ropes. From August onwards the roofing could be supplemented with potato stalks and bracken. None of the huts had windows, proper doors or fires. The only exception being the home of the Village elder which might have a half-door to let in some light and a large stone slab on which a fire could be laid under a hole in the roof. The best seat by the fire reserved by custom for the elder and no-one else.

With shelter and heat taken care of, food in the Booley village was not a problem. Most country folk knew twenty ways of manufacturing milk into something edible, nutritious and tasty, but as was common with a lot of Irish People they loved the milk best when it was sour. From Neolithic times right up to the 17th Century people throughout Ireland would have relied almost exclusively on corn and milk. These were their principle foods before the coming of the potato, and as a food resource was both a healthy and practical one.

One vital commodity was butter, though once the milk had been churned the end result was liable to 'go off' especially in the warmer months. The solution was to bury the butter in the bogs where it would be safe from animals and birds and be kept at a constant temperature that gave the firkin of butter a life of five or even six months, when it could be taken to market and sold as fresh as the day it was made. Though not normal practice there have been cases where butter has lain in the bogs for as long as fifty years after the bereavement of a bachelor farmer, and still come out in a perfectly edible condition. Some experts have claimed that because of the peculiar properties of the bog as a refrigerator come freezer, it would not be unreasonable to think that butter could last as long as 200 years, though no-one has yet lived long enough to prove this!

Other food included bread, pancakes and potatoes cooked on the griddle or in the pan. Fresh meat was not a problem either. The nearby Crinnach River was well stocked with small trout that were caught with horse hair snares or small baskets made of green rushes. And on occasion a cone of paper lined with lime and filled with corn could be an ingenious method of catching Pheasant when the Muckross Gamekeepers backs were turned of course.

But even in a Booley village abstinence had to be observed, and that meant that even out in the wilds there was no meat, eggs, butter or milk on Wednesdays and Fridays, and Mass at the little chapel by the bubbling Gulway river. It could be a hard life for the drovers tending their cattle in the harsh terrain, but it was no picnic back in the village. For here it tended to be the older daughters that were given the task of cooking, tending the sheep, making butter, growing potatoes and knitting socks that could be sold at market.

But it was not all work, for the Drovers observed a custom called 'Transhumance', though the literal translation is based on the seasonal movement of livestock to different grazing. In the Booley Village it was known as a European tradition that had all but died out in the latter part of the 19th Century when young men would visit the and the stillness of the mountain air could be fair ripped apart with the sound of much singing and dancing. Though even this far from civilisation there were still strict rules and protocols to be observed. With the village elder acting as chaperone lest there be too much fraternising between members of the opposite sex. For as the parish priest was keen to preach at every available opportunity, that even though you might be far from the reach of man, you were never too far from the reach of God.

At that time the Catholic Church had a very prudish attitude to anything that involved young men and women. Local dances had to be sanctioned by the Bishop and on the rare occasions when they were actually allowed were so regimented and regulated as to be not much fun at all. Even in the local schools run by the Nuns, it was common practice if a girl turned up in a skirt that showed off her knees, to have a newspaper extension pinned around the hem, even if the girl was only seven years old!

During the summer months, the drovers would drive their cattle up to the higher grazing on the slopes of the mountains, saving the grassland in the lower, sheltered valleys for over-wintering. Up here it would have been only too easy for a cow to fall into a crevasse or bog and the job was a constant strain on tired eyes and patience. The loss of even one animal from the herd possibly having serious ramifications on precious milk yield or surviving a long winter.

Almost what could be described as a nomadic existence, visitors were always welcome, and even a humble beggar or wandering tinker would always be found a spot next to the fire, a crust of bread and a mug of sour milk. Often these men who some would only see as vagrants and ne'er do wells, were the equivalent of the local newspapers and the bearers of up to date news, that usually commenced with the answering of the simple but often used question-come greeting; 'Anyone dead in town today?' A ghoulish, macabre thing to say by today's standards, back then a hard life took its toll on the population and life expectancy was a lot less than today. Effectively cut off from their family and friends for six months, the drovers might go several weeks without hearing any news and still living in times when famine and privation were very much a fact of life. Knew equally well that a recently deceased villager could easily be a friend or relative.

The practice of offering shelter to travellers was a common one and not just in a Booley village. After the years of Famine there were often more than just tinkers and beggars on the road. Circumstances often resulting in tradesmen, schoolmasters, poets and musicians travelling from village to village in the hope of some work and food or shelter in return. Though in most instances all were welcome, as every stranger had some news to impart, musicians were much favoured as they could shorten a long winters night and through song or even dance add some sparkle of cheer to a hard existence. But most welcome were the storytellers, men who might have been scholars or not, but who had the 'gift of the gab'. The ability to breathe life into tales of life, death and history and could for the price of a meal and a dry bed, transport people who's horizons might never reach beyond the next town to far away places and far off times. In a time when many country folk could neither read nor write, had probably never seen a book other than the Bible. A time before televisions and radio's, these men were sometimes the only source of entertainment and education for a people whose very traditions aspire towards words and poems and songs. That so many great writers, poets and musicians have come from Ireland hardly a mystery when you consider the respect shown men who in any other country, would have been regarded as outcasts, vagrants and 'good for nothing'.

Past the site of the 'Booley village', near the 'Cores Cascade' at a point where the Crinnach river drains from Lough Keal there used to stand an old, apple tree and it was here that the men of Kenmare would hand over coffins for internment in the Muckross Friary Graveyard.

It shows both the respect for the dead and the determination of the pall-bearers when you realise that it was a 12 mile journey to here from Kenmare. An arduous journey along a road that as we know, winds its way through some harsh terrain that showed little respect to the procession that would accompany the bodies. Even as recently as the 50's, it wasn't uncommon for a funeral cortege of a hundred or more people, young and old to make the 12 mile trek to pay their respects and honour Irish tradition. It was only with the coming of the motor car that mourners, when offered a less arduous journey to say goodbye to loved ones, took to the new road and abandoned the old. Though some would see this as progress and easier on the feet and knees of the cortege, others might see the strain on the bodies of the living as the utmost mark of respect for those who were making the journey for the last time.

But, back in the 19th Century, just making it to the apple tree was not a guarantee of entry to the graveyard. Then as now space for graves was in short supply and apart from the ignominy of not being able to lay a relative to rest there were also occasional fights between rival funeral corteges and even some moonlight shenanigans that were hardly in keeping with the internment of the remains in consecrated earth. Needless to say, not all those that wanted to be laid to rest in the sacred grounds of the Friary got in and Sir Walter Scott on a visit to Kerry was said to be most offended by the sight of human skulls and bones on the walls of the Abbey, which was as close as some poor sinners got.

Though the desire for a family to have a loved one laid to rest in the Friary grounds was understandable, some other customs regarding death and burial were not. On the Beara peninsula in the 19th Century, it was the custom when a Lauragh woman, who had been married in Adrigole and died childless after her husband was buried, was not, as is the usual practice, interred beside her husband but back in her native Lauragh. The custom compounded by the fact that the Corkmen who carried her body back, had to leave the coffin for collection on the Cork-Kerry border by Kerrymen. If the Corkmen took as much as a step over the border they would be cursed with nothing but bad luck for the rest of their days.

Continuing along the old road, we soon pick the Owengarriff River which, fed by the Devil's Punchbowl high up on Mangerton gains in volume and speed until it reaches the Torc Cascade and plunges sixty feet over precipitous rocks to the valley floor and thence on into Muckross lake. On any day of the year it is an impressive sight and on the rare days when the river is swollen with heavy rain, truly lives up to its reputation as one of the finest waterfalls in all Ireland. The roar of the falling water as impressive as the spectacle itself, the crashing water a stern reminder of the power of nature in a wild landscape, while the sullen thunder that reverberates from the cascade is perhaps also a reminder that close to this spot in 1263, the McCarthy's defeated the invading Normans at the battle of Tooreencormick.

It is at this point that the old road ceases to be a discernable track with its own course through the landscape and converges with the New road that winds its way along the shores of Muckross Lake through a pine forest under-planted with rhododendrons, these plants just like the Japanese deer that can often be seen in the trees are not native to Ireland but were imported from Asia in the 19th Century. Very similar to a native plant that had all but died out by 1800; these plants took to the acid Irish soil and spread like wildfire, quickly becoming a prominent feature of the landscape and a welcome splash of vivid colour in late spring. In amongst the trees to your left is the impressive Muckross House and a mile further on the Muckross Friary that was so prized by Kenmare widows and mourners. Though a ruin since 1652 when it was burned by Cromwellian Forces, the Friary or Abbey as it sometimes called is a place of serene calm and rare beauty and has been a place of quiet contemplation since the 19th Century when many notable writers and artists would visit the site and feed off its beauty and history.

Though from here walkers have to compete with motor cars, coaches and jaunting cars it is a relatively short hop across the river Flesk to Killarney. Considering the staggering beauty and history that is connected to the old road you would be forgiven for thinking that it might be more popular than it is and wonder why the Gowlane Crossroads and the Esknamucky Glen isn't crowded with tourists. The answer is simple enough, you cannot drive along it. Though the lower reaches can be accessed by car, most of it cannot and as long as that remains the case, the old road will remain one of those 'secret spots'. Somewhere where those that know can escape the mad world, the pollution and the over-crowded towns and cities can live on fresh mountain air, spring water and solitude. Not to mention that 'full Irish' breakfast you'll be glad you had as you stand atop Mangerton Mountain and feel like the whole of Ireland is laid at your feet.

CHAPTER SEVEN.
Cardinal Rinuccinni - Sir William Petty - Reencallee Bogs

During 1645, there was much unrest in the Catholic regions of Ireland and an upsurge in what was known as the Protestant attitude. Pope Innocent X was very concerned with the religious problems this was causing and so despatched the Papal Nuncio, Cardinal Giovanni Battista Rinuccinni. A fifty year old Archbishop and a Prince of Fermo. He left Genoa in the spring of 1645, passing through Paris after a meeting with Cardinal Mazarin, who provided the Nuncio with a frigate called 'The San Pietro'. They sailed from Ushant, narrowly evaded a British frigate off of Finisterre and landed on the 27th of October at 'Ardtully Castle' at the head of the Roughty River. (The castle had been built in 1255, was once occupied by Anglo-Normans and was later destroyed by Cromwell's troops in 1653.)

The Nuncio had brought with him the equivalent of £20,000 in six large trunks of Spanish gold and also a considerable number of men and weapons. This was never meant to be a peaceful mission, the 'San Pietro' carried 21 cannons and the accompanying frigates in the Cardinal's large force included 6,000 men, 500 Petronels (a 15th Century fire-arm about the size of a horse-pistol), 2000 swords and 20,000 pounds of gunpowder. Appearing not dissimilar to a small Army, it was no wonder that the British Frigate gave chase, taken prisoner the Nuncio might have proved to be a valuable hostage securing a large ransom. But luckily for the Cardinal it was a clear day and the British efforts to intercept were scotched when an accident in the Frigate's galley caused a serious fire, leaving the Nuncio and his army to sail up the Kenmare Bay.

Kenmare at this time was barely a village, very isolated and it is said that the Cardinal landed first at St.Finians Church where he served mass in return for a safe journey. The boats would have then made their way up river at high tide and berthed at ArdTully which was a well-provisioned fortress owned by the Orpen family.

But Rinuccini was on a mission and he left soon after, crossing over Mangerton into Killarney and from there on to Bunratty Castle, three miles from Limerick city, where he and his party arrived seven days later. At the time it was the imposing home of the O'Brien's of Thomond and the Papal Nuncio was impressed, writing that; 'Bunratty is the most beautiful spot that I have ever seen. In Italy there is nothing like the grounds and palace of Lord Thomond, nothing like its ponds and park with its 3000 head of deer.'

But, even in such a beautiful location, there was no time to linger and after a short rest the Cardinal and his party pressed on the 80 miles to Kilkenny, which was then the headquarters of the Confederation of Irish Catholics. This was basically a union of the 'old Irish Catholics and the Anglo-Irish Catholics' and the Nuncio's visit served only to remind the two camps of their historic distinctions and lead to the splitting of the 'Romanist's' into such factions that would ultimately contribute to their ruin. In no time at all the Confederation had split into the two old camps. The Anglo-Irish concluding a treaty with the English Viceroy, the Duke of Ormonde. This was the main branch of the Butler family who were the major power in all Ireland.

Cardinal Rinuccini supported the old Irish and their brilliant leader, Owen Roe O'Neil, but did try to maintain dialogue with the Anglo-Irish in the best interests of Church unity. But eventually Rinuccini had to break openly with the Ormonde faction, denouncing them in disgust before he left Ireland from Galway in January 1649. To be fair to the Cardinal, part of the problem was his lack of understanding of Irish affairs. But then over the centuries almost all that have invaded these shores have been faced with the same problem and some have claimed that this would not be half as bad, if the Irish perhaps understood themselves?

When Ardtully Castle was demolished by the Roundheads in 1649 it was claimed to be connected with the Nuncio's visit, for Cromwell was determined to destroy anything connected to the Catholic Church and the Cardinals visit, however brief was all the justification he needed.

Many years later Ardtully House was built on the same site, a fine country mansion with features that resembled the old castle it too was destined to be sacrificed on the altar of politics and was burnt to the ground in 1922 at the height of the troubles.

Though today it is but an empty shell, much overgrown with trees and ivy that all but hide the scars, the ruin does have a certain charm and beauty. The house's setting in the lush green foliage alongside the Roughty River offering the artist a perfect painting, and the poet a perfect spot for quiet contemplation. Who knows on a perfect day with the sun falling golden on the broken stone it wouldn't be unreasonable to perhaps imagine the good Cardinal, resplendent in his scarlet robes gazing out in quiet reflection on the Kilgarvan countryside? All things are possible, Ireland is a land steeped in History and perhaps the Nuncio left his mark, like many have before and since.

Oliver Cromwell certainly did. His reign as 'Lord Protector' left an indelible mark on Ireland and Britain and while the history books might claim that he did some good in Britain. The only legacy he left behind him in Ireland was destruction, devastation and death, barely a county not drenched with the blood of the innocent people whose only crime was to be Irish and Catholic.

But not everyone connected with Cromwell was cut of the same puritanical cloth; some brought with them much needed, new ideas about agriculture and housing. One such man was William Petty (1623-1687) born in Romsey Hants, Cromwell's Surveyor General, a friend of Samuel Pepys, a professor of Medicine, a professor of music, statistician, economist, demographer and a founder member of the Royal Society. He had begun life as a humble cabin boy but being short-sighted found the relentless plying of trade between England and France too hard and curtailing a career at sea went into business back on dry land. He did very well, a man of attractive personality and inexhaustible energy he was also ruthless and dishonest. But offset his business acumen with great intelligence and even invented a paddle boat and a 'double-bottomed' boat which might not have been too successful as it was lost in the Bay of Biscay. While in Ireland he invented a 'pacing saddle', carriage that was designed to travel over bogs and rocks. As Doctor William Petty he was a professor of anatomy at Oxford, was a prominent member of the Irish College of Physicians and was instrumental in introducing 'The New Scientific Anatomy' written by William Harvey (1578-1657) the man who discovered blood circulation in the human body.

Petty also had time to produce a dictionary of useful words and was once said to have revived a woman who had been hanged for the murder of her child. He was then given the job of surveying Ireland for Cromwell and assisted by Danish labour produced the Downe Survey, the precursor of six inch mapping.Given the terrain and an area of over two million acres, his maps were very accurate and as a reward he was given 121,349 acres or 190 square miles in part payment.

For the new map, William Petty surveyed forfeited lands in Kerry in the Barony of Magunihy covering 50,000 acres and in December 1654 began to survey the island of

Cappanacush in the Kenmare Bay just off the north bank of Templenoe where he discovered grey marble. Close by he then found white and black marble interspersed with yellow, green and purple on Dunkerron Island and soon became the first man in Kerry to think about utilising the marble as a valuable resource. For many years those with an eye for profit, knew that Kerry's wild beauty was not just that which existed on the surface. For many years, lead ore from the barony of Glanerought (one of the 8 baronies of Kerry) which contained as much as 30% silver in every ounce, had been sold to the Dutch who were willing to pay a high price and had the means of extracting Irish silver.

In 1662 he was knighted by the 'merry Monarch' Charles II, no mean feat for a prominent member of Cromwell's inner circle and in 1670 on the land assigned him by the English government, Petty founded a colony at Killowen with about 75 fighting men who had to go about their duties with literally swords in hand, as a resentful local population made repeated assaults on the colony. In spite of this almost constant aggression, Petty and his men were able to establish a prosperous Pilchard fishery at Killmakilloge, his first Iron smelting works at Gortamullen and the town of 'Neideen' now called Kenmare.

The town was established on his existing land. This was land that the crown deemed had been forfeited in 1659 and should be confirmed to him forever, as well as additional land that Petty had acquired on his knighthood. 30,000 acres of land that had been confiscated from O'Sullivan Mor in the Barony of Glanerought, which covered all lands adjacent to the River Roughty and the site that is now Kenmare.

With his extensive lands and powers, Petty established many Iron works in South Kerry, one fine example in Blackstone Village near Glencar highlighted the problem that faced all his furnaces and caused much resentment amongst the local population. Namely the decimation of woodland to supply timber for the furnaces, though Petty was keen to point out that the de-forestation provided more land for grazing and that the grazing in turn suited the hardy, black, Kerry cows. Locals were not convinced, with Petty's men burning every bit of timber they could get their hands on, there was precious little left for locals to use as fuel, never mind furniture. It sowed a seed of unrest that led to continued harassment of the English contingent. But even these did not deter Petty from another of his 'good idea's'. Considered by many transgressors on Irish soil over many years, this was something that covered many differing elements appertaining to Irish culture and tradition, but tended to be known as 'The Irish problem.' Though when you look back the problem tended to be that the English in particular did not understand the Irish, it never stopped men like Petty coming up with ideas that would alleviate this situation.

Petty's idea was simple to take 20,000 Irish women, the same number of male English immigrants and in one fail swoop ensure that the next generation of Anglo-Irish were raised as loyal English subjects. For a man of great intelligence and experience, it was not one of his best plans and thankfully it never got beyond the speculative. Which, given the Irish, or was that the English problem? Was actually a good thing.

Not a man to dwell on his failures or rest on his laurels in 1672 Sir William Petty wrote his 'Political Anatomy of Ireland. A detailed volume that recounted much of what he had learned during his time as Surveyor General and since as a significant Landholder. Amongst many facts, Petty estimated that wars had reduced the population of Ireland from 1,466,000 in 1641 to just 616,000 in 1652. Of those that were left, three quarters of the population existed on a diet of milk and potatoes and lived in humble cabins with no chimney, door, stairs or windows. This led

Petty to rationalise in 1672 that;' with thoughts of their terrible predicaments, so they will never rebel again.' They were words that were to come back and haunt the English colony for in1688, just a year after William Petty's death, the English Immigration came to an end, after repeated attack the colony was besieged by an army of over 3000 Irish on the small peninsula of Killowen. They made a brave stand, but with odds of 40:1 against them they had little choice but to capitulate. The survivors escaping on two small ships of only 30 tons apiece where they were packed like sardines for an uncomfortable two week voyage to Bristol.

The colony was re-established during the reign of William III, the pacification of Ireland making it safe for Englishmen to return and soon the Fishery at Killmakilloge was thriving, as was the Iron smelting. But the need for furnaces to be kept burning day and night was having a drastic effect on dwindling supplies of local timber and after it ran out the furnaces went out as well.

The legacy of Petty's ironworks still visible on the landscape of South Kerry to this day.

Before Kenmare, or even Neideen, the area where the Sheen River joined the Roughty was called 'Ceanna Mara' which translates from the Irish as 'the head of the sea' and would have dated back to the days of the early Irish Saints. This area is currently the site of the Sheen Falls Lodge, a country house and estate that was once owned by Lord Bruntisfield and was, as we now know, once the site of an ancient settlement and is adjacent to the Old Kenmare graveyard which contains the remains of St.Finians, an 8th Century Church, named after a saint that was as well known for his building works as his good ones. Just behind the ruins of St.Finians, there is a small opening in the stone wall, and a small path that takes you down to the banks of the Roughty River. Here a few yards upstream, at low tide, lies St.Finians Holy Well, a shrine that in days gone by, Local people thought to have blessed waters that were especially helpful to the healing of eye afflictions.

Looking across 'The Sound' from the well you can see Killowen Church on the Kilgarvan road about a half mile outside Kenmare. Though also in ruins it is not quite as old as St.Finians. Originally it was known as Neideen Church and its roofless tower stands over a predominantly Protestant Graveyard full of many English names and titles. It is reputed to have been built around the time of Sir William Petty and would have been at the heart of the English colony before the town of Kenmare sprang up just down the road.

Though Kenmare old and Killowen graveyards represent different faiths, in Kenmare the two faiths have always got on and they are equally as interesting in terms of a social record of hard times past and literally full of history. For a distant relative from England or America this is often the starting point in tracking down a long, lost relative. The local practice of including the departed's home town making for an interesting trawl through the headstones. One very distinct carving on a headstone in Killowen for a member of the 'Maybury' family, all the way from Frimley Green, near Camberley in Surrey. Mind you sometimes knowing the family surname and hometown is not quite enough. There was a case some years ago where a visitor from Dublin was asking after a certain Mr.O'Sullivan on the Glengarriff road by the bridge. Not knowing any other details and obviously not familiar with the generations of O'Sullivan Beara's and O'Sullivan Mor's that populate much of Kerry, he was offered the best of luck and promptly told that he would find at least one O'Sullivan in every valley in the mountains and on every street in every town between here and Killarney.

Though a different prospect to the 'Old Road' and a

slightly longer route, the main Killarney Road is one to stir the heart of any tourist, young or old. It commences proper at the Finnihy Bridge at the northern end of the Square. Widening as it passes the Convent of the 'Poor Clare's', then the Sneem turning that takes you off to Waterville and the wonderful 'Ring of Kerry'. It's a good, wide road at this point, a veritable dual carriageway by Irish standards and shows how the Council's Highway Department can when the landscape allows, straighten out dangerous bends and provide a smooth, swift drive into town. Unfortunately it gives little indication of what's to come and should perhaps be accompanied by a sign warning drivers that like wide, straight roads, or like travelling at dangerously high speeds, or have an aversion to cyclists, or have no love of scenery and cannot understand why everybody else is taking their time, to take an alternative route.

As the homes and B&B's become fewer and farther between, tucked away in a hollow on the right hand side of the road, lies the Gortamullen Mill. Now converted into a fine, stone mansion, it was once well known in Britain and America for its fine Tweeds, the Mill making good use of a local abundance of wool and providing work for local spinners, tailors and assisting the prolific sock-making trade, which was once a staple source of income for many families.

The mill got its power from the Finnihy River and after heavy rain it is possible to hear the roar of the rapids, a hundred yards away, just below the mill at a double bend in the river. What the local anglers refer to as 'a good flood' will also introduce a lot of food into the river's flow and make the Brown trout very active for a few days. When they do eventually come to rest in gentle shallows, a favourite spot is the 'Two Mile Bridge'. This is where the Killarney Road crosses the Finnihy and where in turn, the river drains the Reencallee Valley and it's tributaries with names like 'Letter-south, Carrig-east, Gortamullen and Rencallee itself.

This valley, stretching all the way from Dunkerron to Molls Gap has traditionally been the main source of Kenmare's fuel supply and is referred to locally as just 'The Bogs.' Here in a landscape dominated by a mass of decayed, partially carbonised vegetation and a lot of water, that some say is the sweat of the people that have been cutting the turf for centuries. Men and women still come from mid-spring onwards to cut the turf and stack it into neat piles to dry. It's a process that is totally dependant on the weather and after a bad, wet winter it's not uncommon for the turf cutting to be delayed until July. Even in a well-drained bog, water is the real problem. Turf, or what people in England call Peat, is almost 90% water. It makes for a difficult, hazardous job, just cutting the Turf a real challenge when you are stood on a narrow, slippery ledge on the edge of a bog that legend claims is always bottomless. It's a skill that in an area with few real alternatives, no coal and limited stocks of timber, was vital to a family's survival and one that would have been passed on from father to son, it's importance as real a legacy as any possession. The tool used to cut the turf is a specially adapted, long-handled spade called a slaun, and a really good 'slaunsman' will be able to cut long, even slices of turf and throw them up onto the bank in a single move. If it's a fine day, he will be able to cut up to 3000 sods in a day which amounts to about four tons of fuel, no mean feat when you remember that the turf has to dry out and that a ton of turf will yield only three hundredweight of fuel.

Then there is the stacking. This is another skill that has to be got right, the turf is useless as a fuel until it is thoroughly dried out and the process can take a number of months even when it's done properly. A proper stack of turf resembles an architectural pyramid and will actually let the rain run off; a bad stack of turf is no more than an untidy heap and will stay almost as sodden as the day it was cut.

A good, dry summer is the only way to get the best fuel

and a good, crisp turf that will burn as well as coal or wood and give off that sweet aromatic smell that is evocative of old Ireland and still a feature of even the most modern council houses and bungalows, or anywhere that retains an open fire. This is the reason that houses equipped with the best central heating systems, still have a 'Turf shed' out back, with the crisp, brown turfs neatly stacked beside the oil tanks and gas bottles.

Back in the 60's progressive councils built new homes without flues or chimneys, unwisely believing that there would be no need for primitive open fires when you had oil-fired central heating. What they didn't reckon on was the rising cost of oil, traditional attitudes to heating and cooking and the lure of the open fire. Before long all new houses had proper chimneys and some of the others were converted to accommodate proper fires. It made sense, even oil-fired heating relied upon electric and power-cuts were not un-common. In Scarteen Park in Kenmare, new houses built in the 70's had a back boiler that relied on a turf fire to heat the water and radiators. A system that was cheaper, more reliable and more logical as the bogs were still a whole lot closer to people's homes than the oil depot's in Cork or Killarney.

Another fuel that came from the bogs was 'bogwood' or 'bog-oak'. Quite simply timber that had become part of the process of nature either by growing near to, or falling into the peat-bogs and then over a number of years becoming preserved and sculpted by the swamp process. Some pieces of Bog-oak were large enough to be made into furniture or roof timbers, while the smaller pieces could be carved into ornaments or just burned. Bog-wood was essentially just a by-product of the turf-cutting, in that large pieces of wood once located in the soft peat with long probes, would have to be removed to make the cutting of the turf easier.

Not as reliable or abundant as the turf it was a resource none the less and once that could be used to good effect in a number of ways, whether as fuel, chair or ornament it showed the way in which country folk used whatever came to hand and unlike some of their modern counterparts, wasted nothing.

In 1920 8,000,000 tons of turf was cut in Ireland by hand and Kerry was the third largest peat producing county. Though modern methods have been devised to mechanise the process and increase output so that peat can even be burned in specially made power-stations in a lot of areas it is still more efficient and practical to cut the turf by hand and peat bogs are still as familiar a sight today as they ever were.

But the taking of natural resources from Mother Earth is not without a price and aside from the strenuous labour that was required to cut the turf there was also an element of danger present in every working day. Though perhaps not as dangerous or claustrophobic as working the coal mines of Yorkshire, Lancashire or South Wales where loss of life was an occupational hazard. The Kerry bog lands could in extreme circumstances be just as treacherous and the loss of life just as catastrophic.

So it was on the Monday morning of December 28th 1896 that a terrible tragedy befell the Donnely family home at Quarry Lodge, Rathmore in East Kerry. Close to a station on the main Dublin to Tralee railway line and a place where five roads meet.

It was a dark, moonless night and it had been raining for some time when in the early hours the bog started to move or slide towards the Ashanacree River over a mile away. It is a rare phenomenon, similar to a mud slide and once the tract of bog is in motion it moves with terrific speed, engulfing all in its path. For Cornelius Donnely, a quarryman in Lord Kenmare's Limestone quarry, his wife and their six children, three boys and three girls, there was no time to know what was happening never mind escape and their small two-room cottage was overwhelmed with mud to a depth of fifty feet. They would have died instantly, their home and contents then swept into the Ashanacree River and from there into Lough Leane.

Local people said that as the bog slipped the air was filled with a sound like thunder and Farmers on their way to Killarney Fair day described what they saw as a 'Moving mountain of Fire', as subterranean chemicals mixed with the heavy rain and caused a bright phosphorescent glow.

By the time it was over, the bog had travelled nearly a mile and a half and a later report reckoned that 80,000 cubic yards of mud and turf had been displaced. Apart from the tragic loss of the Donnely family, eight farmers were totally ruined and 45 families suffered from damage to land and property. One member of the Donnely family survived, a thirteen year old girl who had been staying with her Grandmother at Knocknacree and the family dog. It was nearly three months before the rest of the family were recovered and their bodies laid to rest in the graveyard at Knocknascoppa.

In the wake of the tragedy the Earl of Kenmare, landlord of the town of Knocknageeha set up a Relief Fund which was well supported by local people and went some way to alleviating the suffering of those that survived. One donation however was not so well appreciated, five pounds sent by Queen Victoria was deemed an insult and promptly returned. Even the poor and dispossessed retain their pride in the face of adversity.

Resuming the Killarney road, we cross the two mile bridge and start to climb. The road winding its way around some challenging hair-pins, past a few family farms and homes. As the road finally opens out and the valley floor drops away, you get your first view of Bourghil, an imposing edifice of grey rock that doesn't leave your line of sight for the four miles up to the gap. As you get higher, the straight, cut edges of the bogs are clearly visible alongside the patchwork of family farms.

Suddenly you are in the mountains, the landscape of rough stone and grass banking upwards on your right, and growing ever more precipitous as the left side of the road becomes often a sheer drop. By the time you are approaching the head of the gap, the road seems almost perched on the side of the mountain, with Derrygarrif looming over you the sheer drop on the left is at least a hundred feet, breathtaking on a fine day, frightening in the wet, it calls for skill, judgement and patience for though it might be one of the narrowest, winding, mountain roads in Kerry it is also one of the most frequented. With cars, coaches and cyclists often queuing up to squeeze through the head of the gap which at times looks barely big enough for a donkey and cart. It's a strange, claustrophobic moment after the open space of the climb, to suddenly find yourself hemmed in by stone, funnelled towards the narrowest of gaps, then you are through, barely enough time to register the gift shop and car park before one of the finest views in all Ireland hits you straight between the eyes.

In a landscape where it is possible to quickly run out of similes like stunning, breath-taking, jaw-dropping and incredible before lunch, the view from 'Moll's Gap' is quite simply spectacular. The sheer panoramic majesty of Magillicuddys Reeks, the Gap of Dunloe and Purple Mountain are difficult to describe in words that do them true justice. To stand at the head of the gap on a fine summer's morning looking north is one of the souvenirs that can't be bought in the gift shop or saved for posterity on film, it can only be taken away as a precious memory and as such maybe only has true worth and meaning when the visitor is not there. When he or she is stuck in a City traffic jam, marooned in an office block or jostling for shoulder space on a crowded platform. It's a view that connects with your very soul, justifies your coming to Ireland and ensures that you will come back.

If the view alone isn't enough Molls Gap also boasts a fine souvenir shop and a restaurant with maybe the best views of any eatery in Kerry, the huge windows allowing the hungry traveller to feed both body and soul and never for a second take their eyes off the mountains that look in places as though they were carved with a jagged blade.

At a height of over eight hundred feet above sea level, it is quite common even in summertime, to view the Reeks wreathed in stratus like clouds that at first sight can resemble snow in the early morning. The strange views it creates reminding you of the height at which you are now travelling and perhaps hinting that up here in the mountains the weather is infinitely more dramatic and unpredictable and not bound by fictional charts or grinning weathermen.

At the head of the gap, just beyond the doorstep of the shop is a T-junction. Most traffic takes the right turn, and pointing bonnets towards Killarney fourteen miles distant stay relatively high up as they twist and turn towards the famous views and lakes. The road to the left will if adhered to, take the traveller all the way to Sneem, but if Killarney is still your preferred destination, but you want a bit more of a challenge and are feeling adventurous. Then travel along for about a mile until you see a junction on your right. Here you leave the main road and drop rapidly down a steep road into the Owenreagh Valley. Turning right you follow the river east along the valley floor and then north to where it joins the Gerahameen River doubles in size and flows on into the Upper Lake. At this point directly ahead of you is Purple mountain that does not, as some believe gets its name from the proliferation of purple heather, but rather because it is actually purple and made of smooth, purple slate.

Here, miles from the nearest town or village stands the National School, a Youth Hostel and a very useful shop. The road even more dominated by the scenery now turns almost back on its self so that you are heading due west into what the survey map calls the 'Cummeenduff glen' or what local people have for many years given the more evocative name of 'The Black Valley'.

It is a name that perhaps gives some indication of the harsh environment, conjuring up an image of the valley so deep and enclosed that in the depths of winter, the fading light barely penetrates the valley floor. Surrounded on all sides by some of Ireland's highest and most rugged mountains it would be a tough place to live, never mind try and eke out a living. At the entrance to the glen and at the start of a four and a half mile ridge of rugged reeks is the 'Devil's Bite', a jagged rock formation that when viewed from the right angle and in the right light, does indeed resemble a point where locals will tell you that the Devil himself once took a bite out of Ireland's highest mountain range.

The Reeks are strictly for the serious hill-walker and photographer and can be hazardous even for the well-prepared. The mountains are steep and treacherous and the weather as you ascend can be un-predictable and as liable to roast the unsuspecting traveller as drown him. For the best photographs, it is perhaps better to come in the spring or the autumn as you will avoid the summer haze that can all but mask the mountains rugged glory. But at this time of year you will be running the risk of the low cloud that can envelope the highest ridges for sometimes days on end.

At the extreme western end of the Black Valley stands the steep slope of Ireland's highest mountain Carraintoohil an imposing 3,414 feet tall. Although some would say that it is not the most impressive of all the Reeks on a clear day its sheer size and reputation speaks for itself and the view from the top is un-rivalled. Laying South West Kerry out before you like a map.

Many have come to climb Ireland's highest mountain including in 1858 the Prince of Wales himself. The most popular route is to start from the northern side, close to Gortbue School, but it is not for the faint-hearted, the ill-prepared or inexperienced climber could experience difficulties even in good weather and there those that have lost their lives on the slippery slopes. In the 1960's an experienced Australian Climber lost his life and even a local Sheep Farmer who knew the area well and still succumbed to the hazards of wet rock and loose shale.

In the Marian year in Ireland it became the custom to erect roadside shrines to the Blessed Virgin and local men inspired by their faith and the challenge no doubt, decided to erect a large wooden cross on the very top of Carraintoohil. Their achievement standing as an inspiration to others and I am sure a reassuring sight for those that make the daunting trek to the top.

The Black Valley is reputed to have only one day of clear sunshine in a whole year, mid-summer's day and though this sounds like the stuff of legend or folklore, it is perhaps not so far from the truth. Because of the shape of the valley and the dominance of the mountains that surround it, all are in excess of 1200 feet, it is a dark place. Even on a summers day there are area's that never escape the persistent shadows of the Reeks and in the winter months when the sun takes a lower arc in the sky and perhaps never emerges from the clouds that haunt the high peaks, it is not so hard to imagine a day where any room in any house would not need an electric light.

To leave the Valley, you head east back towards the famous Gap of Dunloe, from there a footpath leads from the old school past the 'Gentleman's Rock', the 'Madman's Seat', through the head of the gap between the tall ridges of Purple Mountain and Cnoc an Brahca, past 'Pike Rock', the three lakes of Auger, Cushvally and Black. From there it's just a short walk to the legendary 'Kate Kearney's Cottage, a must-see on the Killarney tourist trail and where the famously tough Kerry woman found the way through the Reeks to Kenmare. Here the scenery runs out and you can follow the shores of Lough Leane back to the main road and from there through the traffic jams back into Killarney Town.

Though a name that is synonymous with natural beauty and stunning views, Killarney itself could be deemed over-rated or even disappointing by those travellers that go there expecting something other than an archetypal market town that it actually is. The narrow streets and awkward layout are in truth not so different to any other stop-over on the 'Ring and the proliferation of souvenir shops can be a little tacky at times. But if you look beyond the crass façade of tourism and take some time to look up above the shop windows, it is possible to see where the true history of the town remains. Many fine examples of 19th Century architecture hinting at the town's long-standing reputation, the queue of 'Jarvies' along Flesk Road a tangible, real link between past and present.

Yes there are a lot of hotels and B&B's and shops and supermarkets and on occasion the traffic crawling along the High street is a nightmare. But if you ever happened to forget where you were, you only have to look up and over your shoulder, only have to glimpse the majesty of Tomies Mountain rising 2413 feet above the town and know that you're somewhere that is renowned throughout the world for its scenery. The name of Killarney as familiar in London and New York as it is in Tokyo.

CHAPTER EIGHT.
'Carrig-a-Caipan'- The Butter Rolls - The Priest's Leap.

Though not quite on the same scale as the magnificent Reeks, Kenmare and its surrounds has much to offer the traveller who perhaps prefers to rest a while in less famous or commercial environs. And in some instances can offer sights that rival the majesty of Purple Mountain and the Gap of Dunloe, not in scale or size but in the realm of unusual or maybe unique ancient monuments.

One such example is the 'Carrig-a-Caipin' which translates from the Gaelic as 'the rock with the cap', an ice-age relic known locally as the Mushroom Rock as with one large stone resting upon another it resembles a huge mushroom or toadstool. It stands twelve feet high with a clearance underneath the cap stone that could comfortably accommodate somebody 5 foot 8 inches tall and keep them dry in a sudden shower. The rock itself stands in an area that was once very close to the Kenmare- Headford Railway line, amidst tree's and bushes and on private land that does much to explain its status as one of Kenmare's best kept secrets.

To visit the Carrig-a-Caipin requires a bit of a trek out of town, down the KIlgarvan road, past the Crossroads and to the next left turn before Cleady Bridge. Here you go along a narrow road for about half a mile past some large limestone buttresses that denote the old path of the Railway. Just past here is a field on the left where the barbed wire fence has been wrapped up to mark the spot and to allow visitors a safer climb over. Beyond this is a straight, grass track about three hundred yards long and at the end of it an old Iron

Gate that allows entrance to the paddock where the rock stands. Because of the dense undergrowth that surrounds the rock, you are entitled to be doubtful such a thing even exists and I am sure that many an uncertain visitor, unable to see anything beyond the gate must have turned back feeling like they'd been had. For the Carrig-a-Caipin is all but invisible until you are literally stood right in front of it.

The first thought on seeing such a natural phenomenon is to ask how it got there. Is it, as some believe, something that ancient man could have perpetrated or is it as most archaeologists believe just a freak of nature? One of those things that just occurred when melting ice many thousands of years ago swept rocks and boulders before it, leaving the two stones buried in thousands of tons of earth until time and erosion swept the earth away and revealed the two stones sat one upon the other. That the Cap stone is a green stone and the one beneath Limestone, further compounding a mystery that suggests that the Mushroom rock was maybe a geological chance in a million and one that will still be baffling tourist and scientist alike for many, many years to come.

Just a short distance away is another curious example of Kenmare's unusual geology. Set back from the Kilgarvan road is an old mansion called 'BeechMount' that was once the home of George McCutchan, rector of St.Patricks. From here if you look on the opposite side of the road towards the skyline you will see a solitary rock. It stands 15 feet tall and weighs an estimated 30 tons and is once again, something of a challenge in terms of just how it got there.

Heading back towards Kenmare, at the crossroads stands an imposing stone cross that commemorates those that lost their lives in the 'Troubles 1921-1922', the title of crossroads one of those Irish eccentricities as it is in fact a t-junction with cottages along the Kilgarvan road and just one other road that takes you down to the Roughty Bridge.

Further on you pass the old KIllowen Church with a

graveyard that might be a film set for a Dracula film, the football field and then the Kenmare Golf Course skirting the sound. The final stretch of the Kilgarvan road opposite the Golf course is perhaps the newest part of Kenmare with large, unusual houses that wouldn't look out of place in parts of Europe or America, a far cry from the mud cabins that would have huddled by the roadside a hundred years ago. A much more fitting house, in keeping with the area is the Shelbourne Lodge, a fine old house situated in a small meadow that was once owned by the Lansdowne family. The garden containing many trees that pre-date the building by a number of years.

Though not a route that can be found in any local guide book, one very popular and manageable walk for perhaps the less energetic walker is; 'Round Roughty'. A five mile jaunt that usually starts at the top of Main Street and heads out towards Kilgarvan on the route we've just done, but in reverse. Ending up back at the 'Irish' crossroads that actually aren't, you take the right turn and head down a narrow road to the Roughty Bridge. Well off the beaten track, the bridge is an impressive double arched, stone bridge at the head of 'the sound' and a spot where, if the conditions are just right, otters can be seen fishing under the far bank.

After crossing the bridge it's a brisk walk along the edge of the estuary to the old Graveyard, then up to the impressively named Dromanassig Bridge. Similar in style to the Roughty, what locals are more likely to call the Sheen Bridge, is a three arched stone structure and a fine vantage point to view the impressive Sheen Falls where the Sheen river drains into the Kenmare Bay. The falls are a totally natural phenomenon caused many centuries ago when the melting ice dragged huge boulders down from the surrounding mountains and with the river in full flood they make for an impressive sight and a mighty roar that can be heard from some distance. The bridge is just a short way downstream from the old Ashgrove Woollen Mill one of the largest buildings in the Barony of Glanerought and for years a ruin with just the sky for a roof. But not for much longer, soon it is to be renovated and turned into an electricity generating station using the Sheen river as a source of power once more. Nature once again benefiting the town and still allowing the river to feed into a calm lagoon where large salmon can be seen basking in the cool, clear mountain water.

The last stretch of the walk takes you away from the river for a mile or so and through a pleasant wood that can be a shady respite on a hot afternoon. Then just as you rejoin the main Kenmare-Glengarrif road you see the Riversdale Hotel on your right. A modern building with a good reputation for accommodation, good food and live entertainment. It manages to sit well in the landscape, affording guests fine views of river and Mountains but not at the expense of those that must look at it. The owners achieving all the practical considerations of a modern hotel, but not at the expense of the landscape that enhances its reputation.

Turning right over Our Lady's Bridge it is then a straight walk up the hill and back into town or for those that feel the need to return to their original starting point via a more auspicious route. You can take the path through Reenagross, up through the back of the Great Southern and find yourself quickly back at the top of Main Street where tired legs can be rested, rumbling belly's silenced and thirsts quenched, safe in the knowledge that you've earned it.

Though on a somewhat more epic scale to 'Round Roughty', another fine trek is the old Kenmare to Bantry road which in 1785 was also part of the main route to Glengarrif. Starting at the Kenmare Bridge the road followed the Sheen river valley to Tullaha where you could carry on towards Bonane a small hamlet with just a Post Office, two shops and a Youth Hostel and from there over Esk Mountain, close to

'Turners Rock, and down into Glengarrif. Alternatively to carry on to Bantry you had to trek up into the mountains to the 'The Priest's Leap' which at a height of 1531 feet above sea level was no mean feat in itself, never mind the drastic descent towards Dromduff and from there along the coast to Bantry.

As stated in Chapter 5, though one of the finest views to be seen anywhere in Ireland, with panoramic vista's stretching as far as the eye can see in both directions. You cannot stand on this high point and not wonder how it got its name for even in a landscape where natural drama and history vie for dominance around every turn, 'The Priest's Leap' has a drama all of its own. The answer to your question however is not far away. For if you look at the iron cross that stands on the county border between Cork and Kerry, and with a foot in each county, you will see a tablet at the base that tells all. That it contradicts what you'd been told on page 42 one of those Irish quirks that makes Ireland a haven for speculation and a frustration for facts.

In 1602 during the defence of the O'Sullivan Beara Castle at Dunboy, two miles from Castletownbearhaven. A Jesuit priest, one Father Archer was en-route to the castle and crossing the mountains to the north of Bantry when he was spotted by enemy soldiers and chased to a point near Knockboy Mountain, where the Priest had no choice but to leap from the rocks which now holds the cross. His faith, good fortune and not a little bit of legend carrying him away from the soldiers, to a landing within a mile of Bantry Town. This version, though fanciful, has a similar ring to that recounted in Chapter 5, while another tale however and one that is certainly no legend, tells of Rector Fitzgerald Tisdale, rector of Templenoe and Kilcrohane in the parish of Sneem and a former curate in Kenmare, who was mysteriously killed at the Priest's leap on Easter Sunday in 1809. All three stories give credence to the name of the spot, that two are legend and the other is tragic fact the sort of anomaly that makes Ireland what it is, an irresistible mixture of folklore and history and views and opinions that can often justify the stretching of a truth for whatever reason.

For those that don't need to trek as far as Glengarrif or Bantry but like a brisk walk through beautiful countryside, well off the beaten track. The old Kenmare-Bantry road can offer another destination at lower altitudes.

Following the Sheen River up as far as Gearha, you look for a left turn. This will take you past mountains with names like Cappagh, Deelis and Coolnagoppoge to the small ancient church of St.Fiachna which is but a ruin surrounded by ancient graves. In a small field close to the crumbling walls lies the Temple Fiachna and in that field lies a strange stone that in archaeological terms is called a multiple Bullaun, but to locals it is 'The Petrified Dairy' or more commonly just 'The butter Rolls'.

The stone can best be described as a boulder with eight smooth hollows around the circumference and sat in each of those hollows a smooth, rounded pebble that looks as carefully crafted as the hollows themselves. In the centre of the main stone is another flat stone with a hollow containing not a rounded pebble but a stone, about 6 or 7 inches long that resembles a pestle. Though the main boulder is as natural a piece of stone as you are likely to find anywhere in the mountains, the hollows are the work of man and suggest great ingenuity and skill. As to their origins and purpose there is still some debate as to whether the Bullaun is a religious or pagan relic and without a specific age or even agreement as to how they were made, no-one is willing to confirm or deny that the stone could have been worked by the Beaker people who were renowned for their great craftsmanship or might even be something as simple and perhaps as practical as the local name for the Bullaun suggests.

Though the facts surrounding the Butter Rolls is

somewhat vague, their value as a curiosity has already established them firmly in local folklore. One local legend claims that the rainwater that collects in the hollows is an ideal cure for warts while another gives the Bullaun a much more religious significance and claims that because it lies in holy ground, anyone who tries to steal one of the pebbles will be instantly turned to stone. The justification for this fable being one of the other boulders in the field that it is claimed is that of a woman who tried to steal a stone, was caught, turned to stone and can only return to her natural form for but a few hours at Christmas.

Whatever your interpretation or understanding of 'The Butter Rolls' there is no denying that the area does have a distinct atmosphere that is similar to that of other ancient monuments or historically important sites. As though history and legend has charged the very atmosphere surrounding the place and left gaps in our understanding. In a world where we might perhaps claim to know everything, it is distinctly reassuring to come across something that cannot be explained away by science, practicality, logic or evidence. Sometimes history can remind us that there is more to knowledge than what you can prove and that the uncertainty that still surrounds many archaeological sites is in itself important. For while we can often determine who, how or when, we might not ever truly know why?

Like many country towns, Kenmare has its fair share of legend and superstition, many date back to times when simple folk were perhaps more ignorant of the power of nature and might attribute extremes of weather or freaks of nature to the workings of Gods ancient and new. Certainly the rise of religion contributed greatly to local folklore and with hardship and death a constant companion for much of the last few centuries, simple folk would do whatever they thought they must to stave off misfortune, evil or death.

One such tradition amongst the poor was the sealing up of a door with butter after someone had died in the house through sickness or other circumstances that back then would have been attributed to the Devil. This involved shutting the door and filling the gap between door and frame with butter that would catch any evil after the soul of the dead had departed. Then the butter would be scraped off and burned in the fire to destroy the evil and protect those that were left. When you remember that at any time Butter would have been a precious commodity to poor people who were often starving, to use it in such a way suggests both their belief in old ways and the desperation that must have driven them in dark, dark times.

Religion too can throw up some interesting superstitions and one particular time of year had more than its fair share, Lent. The forty days before Easter that is traditionally a time for prayer, fasting, penance, abstinence and self restraint. It was also a time when marriage was frowned upon and the Priest was reluctant to even consider the exchange of vows unless in exceptional circumstances. But if it had to be, either as an important 'match' between two families or perhaps because the Groom was headed for America, then it had to be and after the bans had been submitted, the couple would be married on the first Sunday in Lent on what was known as 'Chalk Sunday'. Any bad luck that might be incurred by breaking Lent offset by parishioners placing a chalk mark on the shoulders of the couples as they went to church.

By the time you start heading back to Kenmare it will probably be evening and because of the vagaries of the Irish light and weather, will be the best time of the day to capture those images with a camera. For reasons that cannot be explained even on the most horrendously wet and dismal days, when the rain has been falling like stair-rods since dawn and the roads are running like rivers. Come evening the rain will stop, the sun will return and the last few hours of the day will be so glorious as to make you forget the previous twelve. For then, with the sun slipping ever lower in the sky lengthening the shadows and changing the dulcet slopes of Mucksna from purple to chocolate brown, you can fully appreciate the forty shades of green that makes the landscape such a magnet for artists and photographers alike. The evening light adding a new dimension to every shape and shade and reminding you why the renowned Travel Writer, H.V.Morton would often refer to the 'ever changing skies of Kerry'.

There is something very logical and reassuring about travelling home at the end of the day, as though the very landscape through which you pass is making ready for the coming of night. The mountains metaphorically taking off their boots and stretching out as the long shadows change their shape and the light softens the hardness of the stone. It's a feeling that is bolstered as you pass cottages with the smoke from turf fires curling up into the evening sky, the sweet aromatic scent hinting at fine 'Irish stews' cooked on the open fire and warm soda bread cooling on the kitchen table. The cattle too seeming to know the significance of the hour as they wait patiently by wall and gate for their evening stroll to the milking shed.

But even with the light fading and the day ebbing away, there's still time to appreciate the scenery that has a whole new look in the later light, still time to take a detour over Doughill and through Letter. Still plenty of time to look at the view beyond the old graveyard, the tranquillity of the Sheen Lodge, its orange walls glowing in the evening light and just a few minutes to spy the salmon rising for flies in the lagoon above the bridge.

Then it will be time to press on, to watch the sun sinking slowly into the mountains beyond Dunkerron as you cross the bridge, the fading sun setting the sea afire as visitors squeeze the very last breath from the day by the pier, then wind their weary way back to town for a hearty meal, memories of Butter Rolls, Mushroom Rocks and leaping Priests, and maybe just a drop or two of the Guinness, just to quench the thirst mind…

CHAPTER NINE.

The Famine years - Emigration- The Lansdowne Lodge.

On the outskirts of the town of Kenmare, on the road that comes up from our Lady's Bridge, just past four back to back stone cottages in an area called the 'Bell Heights', is a large stone wall that can seem just like any other wall until you learn something of its history. For though many who live in the town will know it as the perimeter wall of 'Corkery's' Timber yard, some will remember it as a wall that was once part of a soup kitchen in the famine of 1845-1849, and if pressed might even be able to pick out the openings through which the wretched victims of Famine and fever were handed their humble 'stirabout'. A soup made of maize, rice and oats that was for many the difference between life and death and for some poor souls who were too weak or sick to reach the openings no difference at all, their emaciated corpses found just yards from the Bell height or huddled in shop doorways in town where every morning, it was not uncommon to find as many as four or five unfortunate souls who had died during the night.

The Famine of 1845-1849 was catastrophic, its impact on a relatively small, poor country like Ireland as far reaching and devastating as any plague or blight visited on any part of Europe or the East. The hunger decimating towns, villages and rural areas where the potato was the only source of food. It was a cruel indiscriminate killer of young and old alike, a disease that could eradicate three generations in one fail swoop, cost a family its sons, father and grandfather and even its home when rents went unpaid and cruel landlords called in the bailiffs. The Famine degraded and defiled a person and would often just as likely, kil the spirit before the body.

For those that could, the only escape was to leave and not just Kenmare or Kerry but Ireland itself. Tradesmen, clerics, teachers and even musicians had no choice but to leave and with them so too went vital skills and benefits to the community and not least the Irish language which all but vanished in some areas never to return.

But if the Famine was a tragedy then what was going on throughout all this suffering was a travesty. For no more than ten miles from Kenmare in many of the glens and Valleys of Glanerought there was an abundance of Corn. During many of Irelands Famines Corn harvests were unaffected and the British Government saw no wrong in exporting an Irish resource that might have alleviated suffering on a massive scale. Though some historians might at this point remind us that the British were also importing 'Indian corn' or Maize to help victims, it was reckoned that the amount of Indian corn imported over a year was the same as Irish corn being exported to England in one month!

And it did not end there while people were starving to death in Ireland, English traders were speculating on the price of the Irish Corn and when variations in the markets caused a drop in price, it was not uncommon for it to be sent back until the price rose. It has been recorded in some extreme instances where certain cargoes of Irish Corn crossed the Irish Sea at least four times! To export the Corn that might have saved lives was heartless, to then make a profit on the same corn was despicable and shows in cruel and calculating terms what the British Government really thought of the Irish problem and where their true loyalties lay. Not with men but with money.

That Ireland's corn harvest might have fed many of its people was of no consolation to those that were dying in the fields, in ditches and in the towns and villages. For many country folk it was literally the end of the world and visitors to Ireland were appalled at the wretched misery and of travelling through a landscape where there were neither sheep, nor pig, nor cattle or even dogs left.

But, though some landlords certainly exploited and even exacerbated their tenants misery by exporting food, evicting families and doing precious little in the way of charity, many did what they had always done and remained absent. There were a few that did what they could, and alongside Protestant and Catholic clergymen did their level best to assist the fever patients who were but shadows of human beings. The decent landlords gave what they could and would often exist on the same Indian corn so as to spare any other food for the starving. And for many of the starving who had been eating grass and even turf it was often the difference between life and death.

These were dark, desperate times and even in death, the Famine victims were not spared their dignity. Their desperate poverty accompanying them to the grave for when there were no coffins, the dead might be wrapped in straw or committed to the earth in a 'borrowed' or 'sliding' coffin that was used over and over and over again.

William Stuart Trench had been appointed as land agent for the 3rd Marquis, Lord Henry Petty-Fitzmaurice in 1850. Trench had succeeded James Hickson a Dingle man who had been Chairman and Treasurer of a Famine relief Committee and had done much to help Famine Victims. Trench however inherited what was to be a legacy of the Famine and one that faced employers all over Ireland. Namely a severe shortage of able bodied manual workers. There were still reckoned to be as many as 300 victims in the Kenmare workhouse, as many as Trench needed to work the extensive Lansdowne estate and all were too weak or sick to walk never mind do a days work.

At this time the Marquis was more likely to be at ease in his Country Mansion at Bowood near Calne in Wiltshire or in Parliament where he had been Chancellor of the Exchequer in 1806-1807 and was still MP for Calne, and the only way for Trench to resolve his problem was to go to England.

After spending 5 days in deep discussion with the Marquis, Trench returned to Kenmare, but not it must be said with selfish plans for the preservation of the Estate. Instead William Trench introduced a scheme by which any man, woman or child could choose to emigrate to Boston, New York, New Orleans or Quebec and the cost would be met by the Lansdowne Estate. Though the chance of a new life in another country, emigration was not without its risks, the ships that plied the emigration routes to America were not called 'coffin ships' for nothing, as many people that made it to Ellis Island perished en-route and for the survivors the journey might seem only marginally better than death itself. Though many were willing to take the chance of a new life in a new country, many would still prefer to die by the roadside in their Homeland than somewhere in the middle of the Atlantic or on some far flung foreign land. So that in spite of the possibility of a free ticket to escape the hunger, the number of persons in Kenmare in receipt of relief was at its highest point.

In spite of those in authority that were prepared to go out of their way to help victims of the Famine, there were still some that were more driven by money than charity and when the Relief Board itself went bankrupt, the contractor who was in charge of issuing the Indian corn refused to do so until payment was made. Without hesitation William Trench gave private funds from his own bank account to the Board, resolving the matter and it is reckoned saving as many as 1,200 people who were totally dependent on relief and might well have died without food.

It was desperate situations like this and the prospect of many years of continued suffering in the aftermath of the Famine, that finally persuaded many local people that their futures lay elsewhere and 300 were selected for emigration each week. For most this began with a visit to 'Jerimiah O'Shea's' store in Kenmare where helped by the good people of Cork, they were given clothes to replace those that had often been sold to buy food.

But even with the prospect of new clothes and a free ticket there were many that were not able to even consider the 3000 mile trip, men women and children that were so weakened by Famine and Fever that they would be lucky to survive the journey to Cobh, never mind far off America. These were the times when Families were often forced with the heart wrenching decision of sending sons and daughters away to God alone knew what or having them stay and await what at the time must have seemed like an almost inevitable death. Though few parents regretted the drastic choices that were made in desperate times, the letters and parcels that would eventually tell of new lives and new opportunities in a new world were a poor substitute for a mother missing a son, or a sister missing a brother.

In four years 4,617 people left for America and Canada at Lord Lansdowne's expense, but this was not the limit of his charity, for with 3000 people still suffering from the hunger in Kenmare, there was still food to be imported and much work to be done.

Between 1850 and 1851 there were 50 houses built on the Lansdowne estate and most were let, rent free, to families who were to all intents and purposes paupers. Not content with claiming thousands of lives, the Famine had bankrupted those it didn't kill and created a huge underclass of people who had nothing other than the clothes they stood up in, which were often no better than rags. For these paupers having a home was not enough and a great many would leave their homes in March of every year and live what amounted to a nomadic life on the roads of Cork and Kerry, begging what work or food they could to survive the spring and summer.

The bitter legacy of the Famine was in the way that it utterly changed the lives of those that were touched by it, living a life without loved-ones who had died or emigrated almost as hard as surviving the hunger and the fever itself. There are few places in Ireland that don't possess some lasting memory of those dark times and places like the Bell Heights are precious in serving to remind all of us how cruel life can be. But also how, with hope and human charity, man can and will survive.

Not far from the Bell Heights, on the other side of Reenagross and overlooking Kenmare Golf course stands the dilapidated Shelbourne-Lansdowne Lodge, which though it retains some of its elegance and style is like the spectre at the feast or some rambling ghost of days past. Its once proud towers, frontispiece and wings flying in the face of the window tax that was supposed to have limited the fine views of the Roughty River, Knockbrack and Gullaba Mountains.

Inside the Lodge is a magnificent example of extravagant and bold design that would not have looked out of place in any English mansion. Spread extensively over three floors with elaborately carved wooden staircases and exquisite plasterwork, the 24 rooms are a credit to the craftsmen who must have worked with the finest materials that money could buy.

Though the house retains much of its former glory, the grounds have succumbed to years of neglect, the once proud garden wild and overgrown. The small cottage that would have once housed the hardworking gardener in the shelter of the high boundary wall, crumbling and rotting, its roof gone, the ruin left to the mercy of the cruel Kerry skies. The once fine 'hot-house' that would have been the nursery for many plants and seedlings just a shell, the glass that would have warmed and cajoled the seeds, long since broken out and left to crunch and shatter beneath the unwary boot.

In its heyday a huge Cedar tree, the biggest and tallest for miles stood in the grounds of the Lodge, its huge trunk and imposing canopy like a natural umbrella for dance competitions that would be won and lost on a platform beneath its shady boughs. But now it too is gone and like the house, the garden and the orchard full of rotting fruit the grounds are just a mess of tangled thorns and memories.

It is always sad to see something once proud and splendid reduced to a lumbering decrepit shell and as you try to visualize how the Lodge might have looked at its glorious best, you can only wonder about a world that allows something so precious to become just a broken treasure waiting for the wrecking ball. But such is the way of the modern world and only too often it is the past that is the first casualty on the road to progress. Sadly even in Ireland, a country that is ever more in tune with its history and heritage and the need to remember, many fine buildings are being lost to the modern pre-occupation with concrete and glass. Buildings that dominate even intimidate the landscapes into which they are jammed like an architectural square peg in a round whole world. Most modern buildings do not compliment or enhance the landscape or the view, because of their size and design they usually end up replacing or even destroying it. Their harsh juxtaposition against nature an indication of man's self righteous crusade to be always moving forward, with progress and technology an all-purpose justification for the benefits of a progressive society.

But, to move forward and pay no heed to what is behind you is a recipe for disaster and as architects rush to fill our skies with ever taller, ever more elaborate boxes, are they perhaps forgetting the hi-rise hovels that were built in the sixties to replace the slums. Concrete rabbit warrens that quickly became a by-word for squalor and isolation and yet another of those good ideas that people who don't live in a place make for people that do.

In many cities life has become little more than an existence, the pressures and pace of life creating stress that eats away at the senses and erodes the soul. In a world that bends before the mighty motor car, a world of atmospheric pollution, noise pollution and even light pollution it must feel sometimes that there is no point or purpose. In a world of extended shopping hours and 7-day openings it can be hard to know what day it is never mind what month or season when there is often neither tree nor flower to remind. It is no wonder that people are 'cracking up', just as surely as the hi-rise flats they try to live a life in.

In a world where technology and man is the boss, it is therefore infinitely reassuring to find your self in a place where Nature is king and the only power mightier than the earth is God himself. In county Kerry the only Hi-rises are made of stone are called Mangerton, Peakeen, Mucksna, Boughil, Torc and Carrauntoohil, have been around for millions of years and look likely to remain for eternity. Unlike their humble concrete cousins, these Mountains are a part of the landscape on which you walk, they don't enhance or compliment the view for they are the view and their impact on the land will still be there a long time after oil fields have run dry and cars are little more than rusting relics.

In the roads around Kenmare, Killarney and Glengarrif the motor car does not rule the roost, it like man has to fit in with the landscape and sometimes almost gives the impression of a natural conspiracy to slow everything down. The roads of Kerry as winding as any you will find, but offering the motorist by way of compensation some of the most glorious and spectacular views in all Ireland. Though it has to be said that those tourists that only appreciate the views through the windows of their cars and whose idea of a great photograph is a stolen snapshot through a wound down window are missing much that can only be appreciated on foot. Indeed much, some would say the best part of County Kerry can only be visited by 'shank's pony' and anyone forgetting to pack their walking shoes will be forgoing views and vista's that no other place in Ireland can compete with.

Kerry is one of the best places on earth for those who truly want 'to get away from it all'. The footpaths and green roads are the means by which visitors can find places and open spaces that are as detached from the real world as you can get. Still valleys and sheltered glens where the silence is almost a physical entity and where often the only sound is the wind in the hungry grass and the distant bleating of a lonely sheep can seem almost like a noisy intrusion on your thoughts. For in Kerry you can hear yourself think, you can find peace of mind and you can hear the silence.

Though some will tell you that Ireland is not a cheap place for a holiday and a tourist town like Killarney is as much a drain on your pocket as the scenery is a lift for your soul and that yes there is a limit to the amount of blinking leprechaun-related souvenirs any man can stomach, never mind all those pearly-white 'Irish Jumpers. And fair enough if you do decide to eat like a king every night, stay in the best rooms in the best hotels and 'do' the jaunting cars and the boat trips and all the tours, you will soon be skint and more than glad of all those little, plastic cards in your slimmed down wallet.

But it doesn't have to be like that. For those with a good night's sleep behind them, a pair of stout boots on their feet, a full 'Irish' breakfast in their bellies and a rucksack thoughtfully provisioned with soda bread, cheese and a flask of tea. The true riches of Kerry and Kenmare await. The Old Road, Macgillycuddy's Reeks, The Butter Rolls, The Mushroom Rock, Reenagross, Cromwell's bridge and the Priest's Leap are there for the taking and just like the icy mountain springs, the green grass and the fresh air they are all free.

Whoever it was that said 'the best things in Life are free' probably spent some time in Ireland, might have even come from Kerry, but certainly knew that at some point or other, all roads lead to Kenmare.

THE END OF THE ROAD.

ACKNOWLEDGEMENTS

To name everyone that contributed to this book either directly or indirectly over the many years it took to research and write, would be a practical impossibility. Likewise to list the countless books and publications that Stanley Goddard would have read from cover to cover on those dark winter nights in far away Farnborough. When thoughts of Reeks and Glens and Valleys would have been as warming as the embers in the grate.

That he gleaned many facts contained in this book from other books is without question. That he learned much more through long, rambling conversations on Main Street on the 15th of August, there is no doubt. As to who those conversations were with, we'll probably never know. Certainly many of Kenmare's citizens were inspirational in this book getting started and their memories and interest would have been crucial in him finishing it. Men like Bobby Hanley, Tom Lovett, Paddy Corkery, Willy Cousins, Tom and James Brosnan, John P.O.' and even the late, great John .B. Keane who Stanley Goddard met on several occasions.

But to then forget the inspiration provided by the beautiful town of Kenmare, the rugged, raw landscape of County Kerry, and especially the magnificent, monstrous majesty of Maggillicuddys Reeks would be to ignore the greatest inspiration, for without the town and the mountains there would have been no walks, no cycle rides, no photographs, no memories and no book.

For those that would like to learn more about Kenmare and its surrounds I offer no recommended reading list or Bibliography, just a recommendation to visit 'The Kenmare Bookshop' at the very top of Main Street or 'McCarthy's' just down the hill at number 22. Mind you if you've just read this, you've probably been there already...?

The photographs on the cover of this book were taken by Stanley Goddard on a 'Leica' camera, in glorious black and white.

The section of Map used on the cover comes from the 'Ordnance Survey Map of Killarney District 1982' and is used with kind permission of 'Ordnance Survey Ireland.' Permit no: 8140.

© Ordnance Survey Ireland and Government of Ireland.

ISBN 141208676-0

9 781412 086769

Printed in Great Britain
by Amazon